CW00566780

INSEAD Business Press

Available titles:

Manfred F. R. Kets de Vries
YOU WILL MEET A TALL, DARK STRANGER
Executive Coaching Challenges

Manfred F. R. Kets de Vries
TELLING FAIRY TALES IN THE BOARDROOM
How to Make Sure Your Organization Lives Happily Ever After

Manfred F. R. Kets de Vries, Caroline Rook, Konstantin Korotov and Elizabeth Florent-Treacy
COACH AND COUCH 2nd EDITION
The Psychology of Making Better Leaders

Manfred F. R. Kets de Vries
SEX, MONEY, HAPPINESS AND DEATH (now available in paperback)
The Quest for Authenticity

Morten Bennedsen and Joseph Fan
THE FAMILY BUSINESS MAP
Assets and Roadblocks in Long Term Planning

Linda Brimm
GLOBAL COSMOPOLITANS
The Creative Edge of Difference

Lourdes Casanova
GLOBAL LATINAS
Latin America's Emerging Multinationals

Rolando Tomasini and Luk Van Wassenhove
HUMANITARIAN LOGISTICS

David Fubini, Colin Price and Maurizio Zollo
MERGERS
Leadership, Performance and Corporate Health

Manfred F. R. Kets de Vries
MINDFUL LEADERSHIP COACHING
Journeys into the Interior

James Teboul
SERVICE IS FRONT STAGE
Positioning Services for Value Management

Renato J. Orsato
SUSTAINABILITY STRATEGIES
When Does It Pay to Be Green?

J. Stewart Black and Allen J. Morrison
SUNSET IN THE LAND OF THE RISING SUN
Why Japanese Multinational Corporations Will Struggle in the Global Future

Michael McGannon and Juliette McGannon
THE BUSINESS LEADER'S HEALTH MANUAL
Tips and Strategies for Getting to the Top and Staying There

INSEAD Business Press
Series Standing Order ISBN 978–0–230–01875–4 (hardback)
978–0–230–01876–1 (paperback)
(*outside North America only*)

You can receive future titles in this series as they are published by placing a standing order.
Please contact your bookseller or, in case of difficulty, write to us at the address below with
your name and address, the title of the series and the ISBN quoted above.

Customer Services Department, Macmillan Distribution Ltd, Houndmills, Basingstoke,
Hampshire RG21 6XS, England

The Palgrave Kets de Vries Library

Manfred F. R. Kets de Vries, Distinguished Professor of Leadership Development and Organizational Change at INSEAD, is one of the world's leading thinkers on leadership, coaching, and the application of clinical psychology to individual and organizational change. Palgrave's professional business list operates at the interface between academic rigor and real-world implementation. Professor Kets de Vries's work exemplifies that perfect combination of intellectual depth and practical application and Palgrave is proud to bring almost a decade's worth of work together into the Palgrave Kets de Vries Library.

---

* Edited by Manfred F. R. Kets de Vries, Laura Guillén, Konstantin Korotov, Elizabeth Florent-Treacy
† Edited by Manfred F. R. Kets de Vries, Konstantin Korotov, Elizabeth Florent-Treacy, Caroline Rook

You Will Meet a Tall, Dark Stranger

Executive Coaching Challenges

Manfred F. R. Kets de Vries

Distinguished Clinical Professor of Leadership Development and Organizational Change, INSEAD, France, Singapore & Abu Dhabi

First published 2016 by
PALGRAVE MACMILLAN

Palgrave Macmillan in the UK is an imprint of Macmillan Publishers Limited, registered in England, company number 785998, of Houndmills, Basingstoke, Hampshire RG21 6XS.

Palgrave Macmillan in the US is a division of St Martin's Press LLC, 175 Fifth Avenue, New York, NY 10010.

Palgrave Macmillan is the global academic imprint of the above companies and has companies and representatives throughout the world.

Palgrave® and Macmillan® are registered trademarks in the United States, the United Kingdom, Europe and other countries.

ISBN 978–1–137–56266–1

This book is printed on paper suitable for recycling and made from fully managed and sustained forest sources. Logging, pulping and manufacturing processes are expected to conform to the environmental regulations of the country of origin.

A catalogue record for this book is available from the British Library.

A catalog record for this book is available from the Library of Congress.

Typeset by MPS Limited, Chennai, India.

To Sally Simmons, who as an editor's editor has contributed much to my education.

Contents

Preface

The more you say, the less people remember.
—François Fenelon

It requires less character to discover the faults of others than is does to tolerate them.
—J. Petit Senn

If you want plenty of experience in dealing with difficult people, then have kids.
—Bo Bennett

One day a Zen master was walking through a village when he was stopped by an angry woman who blocked his path and began shouting at him. "You have no right to teach others! You are just as stupid as everyone else. There is nothing special about you. You're a fake."

The Zen master said nothing, just sat down quietly and smiled. The angry woman carried on insulting him for a while, but when she got no response beyond a smile and silence, she quieted down and left. By this time the Zen master's disciples were also angry, upset by their teacher's silence. Finally, one of them asked why he hadn't responded to the woman's insults and abuse.

The Zen master replied, "If someone offers you a gift, and you decline to accept it, to whom does the gift belong?"

The disciple answered, "To the person who brought it."

The Zen master smiled and said, "That's correct."

If someone is irrational, or abusive, or behaves erratically, you can mentally decline to accept the "gift." Or you can do something that the Zen master didn't—you can welcome the "gift," as it may help you to understand the person better. As an old friend of mine used to say, "Always welcome the neuroses. They can provide you with a wealth of information." And I agree with him. What I have learned from dealing with difficult people is that they can teach you new skills or provide new insights.

I have written this short book on executive coaching for two main reasons. First, I want to help aspiring coaches to deal better with people who aren't only hard to read, but may also drive them crazy. There are more of these people around than you might imagine. But paradoxical as it may seem, their off-putting and even toxic behavior actually gives us the tools we need to deal with them. In their own mysterious way, they draw attention to areas of their personality of which they're only dimly aware themselves.

Second, executive coaches have to deal with people whose difficult, erratic behavior impacts on the happiness and performance of others in their work environment. The larger context in which they operate increases the urgency to help them create change. From my own experience, I know that if toxic behavior is allowed to continue unchallenged and unchecked, the organization suffers. Toxic behavior has a contamination effect that can ripple through an organization, in the process incurring many hidden, unforeseeable costs. And unfortunately experience has also shown me that the degree of toxicity you see is often only the tip of a very large iceberg.

As many of you will know first-hand, coaching clients can demonstrate a wide range of difficult behavior: rudeness, yelling, shunning, gossiping, manipulating, backstabbing, scapegoating, giving the silent treatment, harassing, whining, ignoring directives they're given, and sabotaging the work they're expected to do. This list is far from exhaustive. These kinds of behavior can cause a great deal of grief, not least to the coach. We have to remind ourselves, when we get upset about their behavior, that it has more to do with them and their problems than with us. But even so, and after many years of practice, I can still find it hard to handle myself in a cool, calm, collected manner when I find myself in these situations. There have been many instances when my clients' behavior has left me seriously emotionally and physically drained.

Throughout my career as an executive coach I have tried to avoid the traps set by difficult clients and I have found that it is easier to do so if I pay attention to my own feelings of hurt and anger. I have become better at harnessing my own emotions when dealing with difficult people and conflict. I have become better at resisting being drawn into becoming an inadvertent participant in a "duel." I always try to keep a modicum of control and resist the urge to try to win an argument. Long experience has taught me that it's always much better to listen. Listening and asking questions leads others to their own, better conclusions. Through the questions I ask, I can help my clients recognize the issues they struggle with.

I haven't always found this easy. Like all human beings I'm tempted to respond immediately when I am challenged or attacked—to try to state my case or prove my point. However, I've learned the hard way that this isn't helpful. It's not a good strategy to get into fight–flight overdrive. Conversely, by not reacting instantly, by delaying my reaction, I have time to think before I speak. As an executive coach, I'm always mindful about what's happening to me. I have learned to pay attention to whatever emotional issues emerge, and not act on them unreflectively. Also, if I delay my reactions, difficult individuals have the opportunity to reflect on the matter themselves.

Every time I demonstrate a willingness to listen with a minimum of defensiveness, criticism, or impatience, I'm giving my clients a "gift" of understanding and also earning the right to have it reciprocated. Suspending my needs for long enough to hear the other person out is part of willing myself to listen. Again, this isn't always easy. But when my own emotions mess me about, my capacity for empathy suffers. My emotions can damage my ability to understand the mental state of others, to listen to them, to feel their pain or joy. To be empathic I have to be able to recognize my own blind spots, the selective filters I use to look at the world. I need constantly to be aware of my own reality, as well as the other person's. I also realize that I can use other filters; that I have the power to view the world through other lenses.

All of us try to manage the cognitive and emotional parts of our brain. They should work in sync. But as coaches, we need to recognize that emotional reactions can get the better of us when we are dealing with difficult people. So, when an emotional avalanche hits me, I always try to pause and reflect. In such instances, I remind myself that while it's important to be able to empathize and understand, it's also important to be logical. For example, each time I deal with a puzzling person, I take account of my own reactions, but I also try to imagine how or what the other person is feeling, and what their take on the situation may be. I have learned that when I'm able to think before reacting (using both sides of my brain), the results tend to be far more positive. In coaching, the reflection–action axis should always be present.

This is not to say that I haven't engaged in some duels over the years, despite my best efforts. I've learned, however, to choose them wisely. I have come to the conclusion that it's not winning these duels that's important, but how many times I have turned away and chosen to look in a better direction. Admittedly, irritation sometimes gets the better of me, and I may get into an argument without thinking it through. But as a rule, when negative (and also positive) emotions emerge, I ask myself questions. I try to reflect on what's happening to me, to force myself not to react immediately. This works well because it forces me to think. This strategy is especially important when I find it difficult to control my own emotions. If my emotions start to get in the way of logic, asking questions has helped me to get back to reality.

Generally, I have become better at not letting my clients get under my skin and sorting out what's me and what's them. Often, difficult behavior has nothing to do with me. So, hard though it may be, executive coaches have to learn to see difficult behavior, of any kind, in perspective, and not to take it personally. While some experienced coaches seem to master the skill of remaining calm in the midst of the storm, others will struggle because of their own temperament. There are very few Zen masters among us.

It should be said that throughout my career as an executive coach I've never met a totally rational human being. All of us, at times, can be somewhat crazy. In fact, many of the "crazy" people I have met in life have helped me see things from a very different perspective. They have widened my outlook. Coaches have to learn to view the "madness" they encounter as part and parcel of their clients' ability to adapt. Madness may actually be what gives them their vitality and originality. Some "mad" people have changed the world. As Seneca once said, "No great mind has ever existed without a touch of madness." My opinion is that too much sanity may be the only real madness. I find it useful to remind myself that I, like all of us, was a kid once—that I once thought anything was possible. I must be mad. Madness is sometimes an appropriate response to the realities we have to face. Isn't it through mystery and madness that we learn what people are all about?

But even where I have had to deal with true craziness, I have always been able to discover some kind of logic. The challenge we have as executive coaches, however, is to figure out what that logic is all about—and that's where the catch often is. Even though human behavior tends to be purposeful, at times it can be hard to figure out the other person's intentions. Fortunately, the behavior of irrational and sometimes hurtful people is often predictable if we already have some basic familiarity with what personality is all about.

This doesn't mean that it's easy to identify the different kinds of personality that coaches have to deal with. Some mystery and confusion will always remain. But the older I get, the more I welcome this confusion. Granted, there have been times when "confusion" has been an understatement. There have been times when I have found myself invoking the serenity prayer of Reinhold Niebuhr: "God, grant me the serenity to accept the things I cannot change, the courage to change the things that I can, and the wisdom to know the difference."

In this book I'm trying to show that coaching difficult people can be an exhilarating experience. Difficult clients have taught me a lot about my own character. Each encounter has taught me something about my own strengths, weaknesses, hot buttons, and boundaries. As the psychologist Carl Jung maintained, "Knowing your own darkness is the best method for dealing with the darkness of other people." I've also learned that if I want to know what kind of person I am, I need only look at the type of people I attract.

In my various roles as an educator, psychoanalyst, executive coach, and even as an executive I have encountered busloads of puzzling people. And as if that wasn't enough, many of my students have asked me to be a kind of Sherlock Holmes and help them make sense of bewildering situations, of people encounters that didn't seem to make sense. I like to think that I have sometimes been helpful. But there have also been many situations when I have been equally puzzled.

In a nutshell, one of the main threads in my work has been to make my students more effective as executive coaches, and that is one of the main purposes of this book. I want to show my readers that they are not alone in their confusion—but that there also will be moments when they will see the light. There will be moments of pattern recognition, some flash of understanding of what they are dealing with.

The impetus for this book was a conversation I had with David Champion, a senior editor at the *Harvard Business Review* (who was also, once upon a time, one of my students), who had asked me to write an article entitled "Coaching the Toxic Leader." Feedback from the magazine's editors was that what I had written was interesting, but it was not a good fit. David asked me if I had ever read *The Screwtape Letters*. I didn't know it, but got a copy straight away. In C. S. Lewis's book—a novel by a Christian apologist—a senior devil, Screwtape, advises his trainee nephew Wormwood on how to secure the damnation of a "patient" by undermining his faith, promoting sin, and capturing his soul. David thought I should use a similar format, while remaining on the side of the angels, to explain to aspiring executive coaches how to deal with some of the puzzling people they will meet in their work. Encouraged by him, I began rewriting and discovered that I didn't really want to stop. What was originally planned to be a short article turned instead into a short book. As well as presenting a number of client profiles, I decided to include reflections on play, authentizotic organizations, and what being a "healthy" individual means.

I have learned not to take things for granted in life. None of us got where we are alone, and this time is no different. In presenting this book, I would like to thank David, who encouraged me to undertake this journey. But I would also like to thank my students and clients, who over the years have taught me all I know.

About the Author

Manfred F. R. Kets de Vries brings a different view to the much-studied subjects of leadership and the dynamics of individual and organizational change. Bringing to bear his knowledge and experience of economics (Econ. Drs., University of Amsterdam), management (ITP, MBA, and DBA, Harvard Business School), and psychoanalysis (Canadian Psychoanalytic Society, Paris Psychoanalytic Society, and the International Psychoanalytic Association), Kets de Vries scrutinizes the interface between international management, psychoanalysis, psychotherapy, dynamic psychiatry, and leadership coaching. His specific areas of interest are leadership, career dynamics, executive stress, entrepreneurship, family business, succession planning, cross-cultural management, high-performance team building, and the dynamics of corporate transformation and change.

Kets de Vries is the Distinguished Clinical Professor of Leadership Development and Organizational Change at INSEAD, France, Singapore, and Abu Dhabi. He was the Founder of INSEAD's Global Leadership Center, one of the largest leadership development centers in the world. In addition, he is program director of INSEAD's top management program, "The Challenge of Leadership: Developing Your Emotional Intelligence," and Scientific Director of the Executive Master's Program "Consulting and Coaching for Change" (and has five times received INSEAD's distinguished teacher award). He is also the Distinguished Visiting Professor of Leadership Development Research at the European School of Management and Technology (ESMT) in Berlin. He has held professorships at McGill University, the Ecole des Hautes Etudes Commerciales, Montreal, and the

Harvard Business School, and he has lectured at management institutions around the world.

The Financial Times, Le Capital, Wirtschaftswoche, and *The Economist* have rated Manfred Kets de Vries among the world's leading leadership scholars. Kets de Vries is listed among the world's top 50 leading management thinkers and is among the most influential contributors to human resource management.

Kets de Vries is the author, co-author, or editor of more than 40 books, including *The Neurotic Organization; Leaders, Fools and Impostors; Life and Death in the Executive Fast Lane; The Leadership Mystique; The Happiness Equation; Are Leaders Born or Are They Made? The Case of Alexander the Great; The New Russian Business Leaders; Leadership by Terror: Finding Shaka Zulu in the Attic; The Global Executive Leadership Inventory; The Leader on the Couch; Coach and Couch; The Family Business on the Couch; Sex, Money, Happiness, and Death: The Quest for Authenticity; Reflections on Leadership and Character; Reflections on Leadership and Career; Reflections on Organizations; The Coaching Kaleidoscope; The Hedgehog Effect: The Secrets of High Performance Teams;* and *Mindful Leadership Coaching: Journeys into the Interior.* Two further books are in preparation.

In addition, Kets de Vries has published over 400 scientific papers as chapters in books and as articles. He has also written approximately 100 case studies, including seven that received the Best Case of the Year award. He is a regular contributor to a number of magazines. He writes blogs for the *Harvard Business Review* and *INSEAD Knowledge.* His work has been featured in such publications as *The New York Times, The Wall Street Journal, The Los Angeles Times, Fortune, BusinessWeek, The Economist, The Financial Times,* and *The International Herald Tribune.* His books and articles have been translated into 31 languages.

Kets de Vries is a member of 17 editorial boards and has been elected a Fellow of the Academy of Management. He is a founding member of the International Society for the Psychoanalytic Study of Organizations (ISPSO), which has honored him with a lifetime membership. Kets de Vries is also the first non-American recipient of the International Leadership

Association Lifetime Achievement Award for his contributions to leadership research and development; he is considered one of the world's founding professionals in the development of leadership as a field and discipline. The American Psychological Association has honored him with the Harry and Miriam Levinson Award (Organizational Consultation division) for his contributions to the field of consultation. In the Netherlands, he has been awarded the Freud Award for his contributions at the interface of management and psychoanalysis. He has also received the Vision of Excellence Award from the Harvard Institute of Coaching. In addition, he is the recipient of two honorary doctorates.

Kets de Vries is a consultant on organizational design/transformation and strategic human resource management to leading US, Canadian, European, African, and Asian companies. As a global consultant in executive leadership development his clients have included ABB, ABN-AMRO, Accenture, Aegon, Air Liquide, Alcan, Alcatel, ATIC, Bain Consulting, Bang & Olufsen, Bonnier, BP, Cairn, Deutsche Bank, Ericsson, GE Capital, Goldman Sachs, Heineken, Hudson, HypoVereinsbank, Investec, KPMG, Lego, Liberty Life, Lufthansa, Lundbeck, McKinsey, National Australian Bank, Nokia, Novartis, Novo Nordisk, Origin, SABMiller, Shell, SHV, Spencer Stuart, Standard Bank of South Africa, Troika Dialog, Unilever, and Volvo Car Corporation. As an educator and consultant he has worked in more than 40 countries. In his role as a consultant, he is also the founder of the Kets de Vries Institute (KDVI), a boutique leadership development consulting firm.

The Dutch government has made him an Officer in the Order of Oranje Nassau. He was the first fly fisherman in Outer Mongolia and is a member of New York's Explorers Club. In his spare time he can be found in the rainforests or savannahs of Central Africa, the Siberian taiga, the Pamir and Altai Mountains, Arnhemland, or within the Arctic Circle.

Email: manfred.ketsdevries@insead.edu
www.ketsdevries.com
www.kdvi.com

chapter 1

Introduction

The greatest deception men suffer is from their own opinions.

—*Leonardo da Vinci*

The man who never alters his opinion is like standing water, and breeds reptiles of the mind.

—*William Blake*

The bamboo that bends is stronger than the oak that resists.

—*Japanese proverb*

So you like the challenge of helping others learn and grow? You want people to be more effective and you'd like to help them change? You are seriously considering becoming an executive coach, or (to put it in a slightly different context) you'd like to be better at coaching other executives in your organization? I must warn you that you are embarking on a challenging journey. As the saying goes, "You will be living in interesting times." Indeed, I am always amazed at the power of the coaching process—it has the potential to draw out capabilities that your clients never even knew were there. But do you understand what executive coaching requires? Do you understand the effort involved? Being an effective executive coach requires insight into human behavior and knowledge of organizations. It also involves patience, stamina, and hard work.

In simple terms, I see executive coaching as allowing clients to pick your brains—it's about knowing how to listen and how to nudge them in the direction that makes them feel at their best. I have found (and this will come as no surprise to any experienced coach) that a great way to have an impact on people is simply by just listening to their stories. By helping your clients create a cohesive, comprehensive narrative of what is important in their lives, and what is troublesome, they will discover things about themselves that they never knew they knew. And while this work is not always a bed of roses, let me assure you that it can be extremely gratifying. To assist people on their journeys of self-discovery—helping them understand what's important to them, what they're good at, what they're not good at, and the things they need to do to be even better—can be exciting. As the saying goes, a mind once stretched will never be the same.

However, you should be aware that the challenge you are up against could be daunting. Opening doors is one thing, but having clients walk through them is another. With difficult people the task can be compared to figuring out a 5,000-piece jigsaw puzzle with a lot of sky—it can be quite daunting.

You should also know that when your clients tell you they want to change, to move forward, this is often nothing more than paying lip service to an idea. They may consciously believe that they want change, but *unconsciously* is a different matter. They are far more likely to want other people to change.

You need to realize that a considerable part of human behavior, if not the largest part, is unconscious. Many people, without knowing it, are strangers to themselves, not really aware of why they're doing what they're doing. Coaches must always be sensitive to the fact that what people say they want, and what they do, are two very different things. In reality, many of the people you will be dealing with are engaged in heroic efforts at self-sabotage, in the process destroying the lives of others and even their organizations.

Many executives lead their companies to success, others drive them crazy, and some do both. As an executive coach you often have to deal with those in the latter two categories. That said, I should point out that working with executives who drive people (and companies) crazy requires great imagination and sensitivity to interpersonal relationships. Having some clinical sense is, in my view, a plus. Given the importance of unconscious processes, many of the people you encounter (including yourself) will have serious blind spots. We all have our darker sides. What we may find in the basement of our mind can be surprising. Skeletons abound. But you shouldn't be shocked by it. It's part of the human condition. It makes us truly human.

The word "clinical" means "at the bedside." It is helpful to point out connections between clients' past and present behavior—after all, the past is the lens through which we understand the present and shape the future. Cognitive behavioral theory has its place, but so has psychodynamic understanding. Good theory, without being dogmatic, will always be useful in shining light into the behavioral darkness.

Many of the people you encounter will be repeating past behavior patterns. Your challenge is to make them realize that what might have been quite useful behavior—even a survival strategy—at the age of 10, may no longer be effective at the age of 40. Your clients, however, may be blind to this. As the writer and statesman Johann Wolfgang von Goethe used to say, "The hardest thing to see is right in front of your eyes." You need to help your clients see that they are stuck on automatic pilot. They may be suffering from developmental arrest. Only when they realize this might they be willing to consider other ways of doing things.

Another advantage would be a solid understanding of what life in organizations is all about. Organizations are complex entities. An effective executive coach needs to understand the way these entities function, know something about strategy and structure, have some familiarity with organizational group dynamics, make sense of an organization's corporate culture, and be able to speak its language. This means that you should always have a systemic orientation when you do your work. You need to understand that organizations are made up of constellations of forces that must be aligned if your interventions are to be effective.

You should also bear in mind that, when you do this kind of work, the boundaries between consulting and coaching can become quite blurred. I believe that executive coaches should *not* be used in a consulting capacity to help weak CEOs. We shouldn't be teachers, but "awakeners"—we should help executives think through and tackle their own problems. I firmly believe that senior executives need to deal with their problems on their own and not get caught up in dependency relationships.

Obviously, senior executives have a considerable influence over the health, happiness, and future of the people who work for them. They can create an environment that allows others to grow and give their best, or they can do the opposite. Indeed, some executives (consciously or unconsciously) create the kind of work environments that poison other people's lives. When an executive's psychological make-up is problematic—even toxic— all business plans, ideas, interactions, and even the system and structure of the organization itself, are in danger of becoming a mirror image of that negativity. Always be attuned to the possibility that a senior executive's toxic behavior can permeate an organization's culture so thoroughly that the people who work there get sick.

I have learned from my work as a psychoanalyst that toxic people have often had miserable experiences in childhood and afterwards that they subsequently act out in the workplace, like a repeat performance. In so doing, they make life miserable for their employees, sowing unhappiness wherever they go. They act out their private issues on a public stage, externalizing their internal world. Sadly, I regularly encounter situations where toxic bosses contribute to extreme stress and even nervous breakdowns—not exactly a prescription for high productivity and morale.

Interestingly enough, many executives are the exact opposite of the rational men and women described in management textbooks. As I have seen far too often, the gap between desired and actual behavior can be enormous. Given how destructive people can be, as an executive coach you need to understand what differentiates toxic executives from more inspirational ones. What makes them so special? What are their defining characteristics?

To help make sense of the difficult encounters you may have in executive coaching, I have put some of these toxic bosses "on the couch," at least symbolically. In the chapters that follow, I describe some of the more puzzling executives I have encountered in my coaching work to help you gain greater insight into what they are all about. Note that this is just a sample—there are many more variants—but keep in mind that "ideal" types are the exception, not the rule. There are not many "ideal" types in our world. As you will have realized by now, *Homo sapiens* is a complex animal. To be fair, most of us are "hybrids." Many of the toxic people I have encountered have the characteristics of various personality types, but are still able to cause serious trouble for themselves and others. They touch others in very negative ways. They are masters of destruction, and as such they're not easily forgotten. They cast a dark shadow that lasts for a long time.

2

The Narcissistic Executive

For the most part people are not curious except about themselves.

—John Steinbeck

I don't care what you think unless it is about me.

—Kurt Cobain

He who is enamored of himself will at least have the advantage of being inconvenienced by few rivals.

—G. C. Lichtenberg

The leadership style most frequently found at top management levels is the narcissist. Indeed, this kind of leader is over-represented in the higher echelons, and derailment at the top is often due to the excesses that come with this kind of behavior. In these instances, position and disposition seem to interact in mysterious ways, resulting in instability. Ultimately the rot sets in.

Narcissism is a psychological condition with a distinct etiology, ways of acting, problems, and benefits. That being said, it is not a disorder that a person either does or does not have. We all possess narcissistic characteristics, but in varying degrees. In fact, we need a modicum of narcissism to function properly—a healthy dose of narcissism is part of the body's immune system, defending it against the vicissitudes of life. It creates the foundation of self-confidence, assertiveness, self-expression, and the proper execution of power. Narcissism enables us to do things, to feel good about ourselves, and to impose ourselves a little. But the narcissistic pendulum can swing too far to one side, creating a personality disorder. Driven by grandiose fantasies about themselves, true narcissists are selfish, inconsiderate, require excessive attention, have a sense of entitlement, and pursue power and prestige at all costs.

To assess whether someone is truly a narcissist, you need access to that person's inner life, which (as you should know by now) is not easy. However, you can observe its behavioral manifestations—and that is something you can work with. Knowing the signs of narcissism helps you to recognize these people; it tells you what you're up against, what contributes to their often puzzling behavior, and how to deal with them.

Children exposed to certain types of parenting—whether it is over- or under-stimulation—can become confused and destabilized. The problem is that some parents, although seemingly focused on their offspring, actually have little regard for the child in its own right; they are unable to engage with it in an emotionally adequate manner. Not surprisingly, this can cause disequilibrium and instability. Such children may become insecure and excessively needy. They do not develop the self-confidence to keep existential anxiety at bay. Instead, they may grow up feeling inadequate or inferior, feelings that will haunt them for the rest of their lives. Due to this basic sense of insecurity, a sense of deprivation, anger, emptiness, and neediness will follow them wherever they go. Hence they will be highly sensitive to any real or imagined threat to their self-esteem, and their narcissistic legacy may turn into dysfunctional behavior.

I have seen how these children hold on to fantasies of grandiosity—"I'm not just all right; I'm the greatest"—setting in motion the psychological engine that drives excessive narcissistic behavior. (You should view this behavioral pattern as a defense against inadequacy—of not feeling good enough.) Throughout childhood, these narcissists-in-the-making strive to marshal support for their grandiose (though tenuous) image of themselves by cultivating whatever good looks they have, learning to charm others, and often just by working hard. Typically, this behavior continues into adulthood, since it's a pretty good prescription for success, but in the process they become fixated on power, status, prestige, money, superiority, and glory.

You should be sensitive to the fact that narcissists' seductive way of operating (as they rise to power) is really pseudo-charm, only used as long as it serves the purpose of self-aggrandizement. People they encounter will be treated as pawns as they work towards success—and that will include you as an executive coach. You may feel exploited and used, but narcissists see themselves as special and consider that rules are made for others, not for them. Their sense of entitlement means that they're prone to outbursts of rage when they do not get what they want. And as their sense of self-esteem remains fragile, it creates conscious and unconscious power dynamics.

Narcissistic executives very frequently create toxic relationships with the people who work with or for them. Their neediness evokes certain reactions from those around them. As a coach, you'll notice that it doesn't take long for people with a narcissistic boss to realize the need to admire and please that person. Narcissistic executives like this kind of admiration. It's an emotional fix; without it they can't function very well. They want others to approve of whatever they do, and they need to be in the limelight. But this form of interaction comes with the risk of creating a mutual admiration society in which everyone only hears and sees what they want.

As an executive coach you should always be sensitive to the fact that candor flees authority. Narcissistic leaders are surrounded by yes-men who quickly learn that when people are unwilling to share the leader's way of looking at the world there is a danger of tantrums. Narcissists tend to see any form of disagreement as a personal attack. Their tantrums should be viewed as a regression to earlier feelings of helplessness and humiliation, which have turned into blind rage, a re-enactment of childhood behavior. The difference is that, given the considerable power they now wield within an organization, the impact can be devastating.

Let me tell you about Simon. When I first heard about him, Simon was regarded as one of the most promising senior executives in his company, although a number of non-executive directors had had second thoughts about whether he was the right person to succeed the current CEO. Would Simon be able to take the company to the next level? Did he have sufficient maturity to do it? Their doubts prompted Agnes, VP of Talent Management, to ask me to become Simon's executive coach, with the aim of preparing him for possible succession.

To help me understand better what Simon was all about, Agnes shared a number of concerns. She started by telling me about a series of rash decisions he had made when first on the job, which were perceived as counter-cultural, raising questions about whether he understood what the corporate culture was all about. Was he really willing to accept their way of working? Did he realize that the rules applied to all employees and that he was no exception?

One criticism was his attraction to deal-making. Agnes told me that he had discussed possible acquisitions with investment bankers, and had embarked on a dramatic expansion plan despite others' cautionary remarks. He had an apparent need to see his name in the press, ignoring the "shoulds" and "shouldn'ts" from the people in Communications. A number of people in the organization viewed him as a "user"; they felt he took advantage of them and that there was a lack of reciprocity in their dealings with him. One person said that he felt like part of the scenery on Simon's stage to success. So the basic question remained: Was he committed to the company, or did he just see it as a halfway station?

Agnes had the impression that Simon felt the rules were for others, not for him. His lobbying efforts to be elected "businessperson of the year" were resented. More seriously, he had decided to relocate the regional head office to a new, more upmarket location. Moving might have been the right decision, given the cramped conditions they had been working in, but the whole exercise had turned out to be a lot more expensive than planned. To cap it all (Agnes began to sound somewhat exasperated), he was leasing a small corporate plane—his rather lame excuse being that it would save money, given the difficulties of the head office connecting to the other offices in the region following the move.

However, it was a series of informal conversations Agnes had had with a number of Simon's subordinates at the company's annual event that had determined her to contact me. They had all gone on and on about their dislike of what was happening at the office. Some of the better people had left for the competition; others had asked for a transfer or had allowed themselves to be headhunted. She (and others) had begun to wonder whether Simon really was the golden boy everyone thought. Would I talk to him about the prospect of starting a coaching assignment?

My first encounter with Simon was pleasant: tall, well dressed, and friendly, with a somewhat flirtatious manner, Simon was very easy to talk to—he didn't hold back, and seemed willing to discuss anything. He opened up about his relatively short tenure at the company, how he had been "poached" from a competitor, adding that the press had made quite a fuss about how costly a hire he had been, amid accusations of excessive pay in the private sector. He said that he had really liked his previous job, but the top job would not have been available to him for some time. This was the main reason that he had accepted his present position.

When I asked how he saw the future, Simon clearly felt that he was a shoo-in for the top job. He obviously didn't think much of the other candidates. He seemed quite confident about it.

As he talked, I noticed the extent to which Simon lived in a binary world, one in which people were either "for" or "against" him. He made it clear that anyone against him should be prepared to be a target. Paranoid thinking is one of the trademarks of narcissists (paranoia rather than gout being the "disease of kings" nowadays). From what I heard from others in the company, Simon was no different. If he were to be believed, there were always people out to get him. During his short tenure he had removed some of the more independent thinkers in his team. Executives who hesitated to take his side were easily transformed into targets for his anger. As might be imagined, this way of looking at the world created a very toxic atmosphere.

As an executive coach you should be on your guard when dealing with people like Simon. Be careful how you structure your conversations. Here are a few dos and don'ts to consider. You need to convey a feeling of respect and acknowledge their need to be recognized and seen as important. Do everything in your power (at least initially) not to unbalance their delicate sense of self. At the same time, you shouldn't reinforce their grandiose perceptions of themselves (which would constitute a denial that there was anything wrong in their way of dealing with others) or accentuate their weakness (which could frighten them). As a coaching strategy, my advice would be to show empathy and gain the narcissist's trust, after which it should be possible to try out "baby step" confrontations of their vulnerabilities.

Clearly, if Simon wanted to have a shot at the CEO position he needed help in understanding the implications of his leadership style and how it was affecting his sense of reality. My "ally" in helping Simon change some of his dysfunctional behavior patterns was his wish to succeed the CEO. It can often be helpful to draw on a narcissist's competitive side in this way, without fueling their tendency towards grandiosity.

By gradually building Simon's self-confidence, I was able to shrink his misguided attempts at self-preservation through grandiose and paranoid actions. In my coaching role, I took advantage of the narcissist's tendency towards idealization. Simon's positive "transferential" feelings towards authority figures (in this instance, me) helped me to establish a more secure working relationship with him. And here it is good to keep in mind that no relationship is ever really a new relationship. All our relationships are colored by previous ones we have had. As a coach, you should be aware that your clients will transfer the feelings they have had about previously important people toward you. But when you are leveraging idealization, always be aware how easily the pendulum can swing in the other direction and how speedily you can be devalued. That said, whatever degree of idealization is in place in this kind of coaching relationship, my advice is to use it to help narcissists like Simon construct a less fragile self-image.

This kind of intervention is not a quick fix. In Simon's case it was quite some time before I saw results. But gradually, as I helped him build his self-confidence, I could see how he became less needy, more prepared to share the limelight with others, more empathic, more effective as a mentor to the people working for him, and more in tune with the cultural values of the company. All in all, his behavior became more grounded in reality. A positive sign that he was on the road to a more stable self was his decision to sell the company plane. And just as important (given his ambitions), the key decision-makers in the company noted these changes and liked what they saw.

To ensure the continuity of Simon's "new self" (and never losing sight of how easily people can regress to earlier behavior), I suggested that he attend a CEO seminar that I had been running for some years. I felt that participating in the group sessions involved would help stabilize his more balanced self-image.

When the time came for the CEO to retire, Simon was indeed selected for the top job.

3

The Detached Executive

I am in truth the Steppenwolf; that beast astray who finds neither home nor joy nor nourishment in a world that is strange and incomprehensible to him.

—*Herman Hesse*

Attachment is the great fabricator of illusions; reality can be obtained only by someone who is detached.

—*Simone Weil*

Detachment produces a peculiar state of mind. Maybe that's the worst sentence of all, to be deprived of feeling what a human being ought to be entitled to feel.

—*James Dickey*

Some people can get very close to others; others find it very hard to do so. If you belong to the latter group, it's likely that getting too close will cause feelings of discomfort. However, it's important to realize that questions about closeness are at the heart of the human condition. Awareness of this is crucial in your work as a coach. You need to be attuned to how the people you coach handle attachment issues and how dependent they are on others for emotional satisfaction.

You must have realized by now that the specific way we interact with others derives from the kind of attachment pattern we have learned to be comfortable with. And as is the case with so many other things, the factors that create comfort and discomfort have their roots in our very earliest years. The template for the kinds of relationship that make us feel at ease is laid down at an age when we are extremely impressionable. To be more specific, it starts with the "dance" between mother and child. The way we relate to our primary caregiver creates a prototype of how we will relate to others. I cannot stress strongly enough that our early mother–child interaction patterns determine the nature and quality of all our present and future attachment relationships.

The ability to form attachments is biologically driven and is part of our evolutionary heritage. *Homo sapiens*, like our close cousins the great apes, is born with a repertoire of instinctive behaviors that help us survive as human infants. For the purpose of psychological and emotional development, as well as survival, both caregiver and infant have preprogrammed, instinctive pathways to foster attachment behavior. Obviously, mothers who respond to their infants' needs and provide security are more likely to have infants that survive, passing on their genes.

Based on the nature and quality of their early attachments, children develop an internal working template of relationships (systems of thoughts, memories, beliefs, expectations, emotions, and behaviors about themselves and others) that will serve as a pattern for all future relationships. How these attachment patterns work themselves out in our inner theater will very much depend on the nature and quality of repeated interactions with our caregivers. These working models of relationships can turn out to be positive (i.e. people can be trusted, confided in, helpful in distress) or negative (i.e. no one can be trusted, people do not really care, one is all alone in the world). Not surprisingly, the same motivational system that underlies infants' attachments to their caregivers also underlies the emotional bond that develops between other people later in life. You should know that as we grow older, attachment patterns are transferred from parents (or other caregivers) to other people in our life. The quality of attachment established early in life will affect future adult relationships, including romantic love, friendships, and workplace behavior.

Securely attached infants, having been exposed to parents who were responsive to their needs, will perceive other people as dependable, caring, and trustworthy. These people consider themselves wanted, worthwhile, competent, and lovable. This kind of experience creates a foundation for a secure sense of self-esteem, incorporating a sense of competence and self-worth, and a healthy balance between dependence and autonomy. It also contributes to the development of empathy, compassion, and conscience.

In contrast, it's also important to know that when their attachment needs are not met, children will feel insecure (a process again later mirrored in adulthood). Growing up with disorganized, absent, non-responsive parents often leads to the development of avoidant patterns of attachment. These individuals have learned as infants that proximity seeking is not enough to draw out satisfactory responses from caregivers. Children subjected to dysfunctional childrearing may feel bad, unwanted, worthless, helpless, and unlovable. Knowing something of their early experiences may help you understand why they see other people (including you, as their coach) as unresponsive to their needs, insensitive, hurtful, and untrustworthy. Many of these people perceive the world as unsafe and life as painful and burdensome.

You should also be attuned to the fact that to get some kind of response from their caregivers, these children may resort to desperate strategies, one of which is hyper-activation and the other deactivation—in other words, activities that focus on moving toward people or away from them. These strategies can be interpreted as exaggerations of primary attachment behavior. Some of these children will be extremely clingy and emotionally needy (always on the lookout for comfort and attention), while avoidant others (who have experienced unsupportive, inconsistent caretaking) may resort to emotional distancing and greater reliance on the self than on others. The latter will have problems with intimacy. They will be uncomfortable when close to others and nervous at proximity.

By detached executives, I am referring to people who don't know how to handle close relationships. They find it difficult to trust others completely, or to allow themselves to be dependent on anyone. Although some of them may want to be closer to others, distancing becomes a defensive psychological strategy. They often show few signs of needing other people, don't bother trying to attract others' attention, and try to cope with problems on their own. They are likely to lack (or not express) empathy, and may even take pleasure in others' unhappiness. They keep their distance, fearful that they may get hurt.

There are two distinct avoidant types: the "fearful" and the "dismissive." The fearful avoid attachment relationships to prevent being hurt or rejected. Although they would like to have emotionally close relationships, they find it difficult to trust others completely or to depend on them. They are unable or unwilling to share their thoughts or feelings with others. They often use excuses to avoid intimacy (such as long work hours or the need to travel). They invest little emotion in romantic and social relationships and experience very little distress when a relationship ends. Other common characteristics include a failure to support partners during stressful times. Empathy does not come naturally to them.

In contrast, people with a dismissive attachment style do not experience any need for closeness, having deeply suppressed their emotional side. They have an extremely strong defensive system that has pushed any of these feelings underground. This is a highly defensive mode of self-reliance. These people tend to be true loners who regard relationships and emotions as relatively unimportant. Their response to conflict and stressful situations is typically to distance themselves from them.

But let me give you an example of how I tried to make sense of one of these detached, avoidant individuals. Our encounter began with a phone call from one of my colleagues, who had been working with a company in the telecommunications industry; she asked me if I could do her a favor. Because she was coaching the CEO of this organization, she was reluctant to get involved with the other executives. However, she knew that Doris, the VP of Information Systems, was in trouble. A number of senior executives in the organization were worried about her and felt she needed help. My first response was to ask my colleague if Doris felt the same way. After a long silence, my colleague replied that she wasn't sure, as they had never had a serious conversation. But given the fact that her responsibilities had been curtailed recently after a number of very questionable decisions, she thought Doris might be willing to consider help. She added that she knew that I was going to make a presentation about leadership coaching and feedback to the senior management of this particular company the following week. She thought this would provide an excellent opportunity to meet Doris and go from there. But she warned me that it would be a challenge. Doris wasn't exactly warm and welcoming. She seemed to be a loner and although she was in her late 40s, she had never been married or (to the best of my colleague's knowledge) ever had a meaningful relationship.

The following week, after I ended the workshop, I managed to have a conversation with Doris. I had seen her sitting in a corner far at the back, and approached her during the cocktail party afterwards. We didn't get off to an easy start. Doris was rather standoffish, initially, but I eventually got her attention once I discovered that Doris was a dog lover. Our conversation moved on from dogs to her career, and after an initial hesitation, she asked me if I helped my clients to get unstuck in their career. When I said I did, she hesitantly told me that things were not going so well for her. She mentioned that she had been doing quite well as a department head, but having been promoted to VP, her new job had become a burden instead of a blessing. The new position had increased her visibility in the company, a change that seemed to have made her very uncomfortable. It had led to a number of conflicts and also a few unfortunate decisions. Things came to a head when the person responsible for HR told her that a number of people in the company didn't appreciate her leadership style. Not long after, she had *de facto* been demoted when a big chunk of her responsibilities was taken away. What troubled her now was that she didn't know what to do differently. What had gone wrong? Her next question came quite out of the blue. "Did I think that coaching would be helpful to her?" You can imagine my response. As the company was supportive of coaching for its executives and was willing to give Doris another chance it took very little effort to set up a coaching arrangement. Our contract was that I would see Doris for 12 sessions, after which we would decide together what to do next.

Let me start by saying that there was much more to Doris than what she could tell me about dogs. When I began to know her somewhat better, I discovered that she was a dreamer with a rich and complex fantasy life. But she was also a very lonely woman. Clearly, her socially and emotionally withdrawn manner prevented others from forming close relationships with her. Her inscrutability did not help. Doris was very hard to read, which made others feel uncomfortable. From what I could see, she seemed to be indifferent to both negative and positive feedback. For example, when I praised her about her previous accomplishments in the company, she didn't really react. This is something that can rattle people.

Of course, Doris was an avoidant or detached individual and, as you can probably guess, they're not the easiest people to coach. I knew from previous experience that avoidant people usually have poor insight about what makes them the way they are. They are also not the kind of people who welcome coaching. They will only ask for help when the disorder starts to interfere with their life significantly or impact it in a negative way. I realized that the only reason Doris was open to the idea of having an executive coach was her demotion—behind her apparent indifference, she was quite ambitious. It was very clear to me that her job meant a lot to her. There weren't many other things in her life.

People with attachment disorders have a great capacity for rationalization— they always have a logical explanation for the way they behave. But in fact, I've found that they're masters at deluding themselves. I knew that if I was going to be able to help Doris prepare for change, a multi-pronged effort would be the most effective intervention strategy. A number of coaching strategies have worked for me when dealing with people with attachment disorders, including psychodynamic explorations, cognitive and emotional restructuring, group coaching, paradoxical intervention, motivational interviewing, and the use of psychodrama (role playing). A combination of these strategies can help break through their defensive structure, and get these avoidant, detached executives to reveal (and actualize) their emotional issues. A word of caution here—clients taking prescribed antidepressant medication can be less sensitive to feelings of anxiety and rejection. Sometimes, a combination of medication and coaching may be more effective than either form of intervention by itself.

Detached executives tend to be socially inhibited and feel socially inept. Because of their feelings of inadequacy and inhibition, they will try to avoid any form of activity that involves socializing or interacting with others. They often have exaggerated negative beliefs about themselves—beliefs that may never have reached consciousness, which makes interventions even more difficult. Doris was no different. She did not have a solid sense of self-esteem. She needed to develop a greater sense of self-confidence, especially in interpersonal situations.

As I do in many coaching situations, I thought it would be a good idea to give Doris some "homework." I asked her to gradually face precisely the kinds of situation that she was most afraid of and would typically avoid. This kind of systemic exposure (by creating structured exercises), combined with reframing their unrealistic ways of thinking about themselves, will set the mind and emotions of detached individuals on the right path. Since they avoid social situations as much as possible, their people skills (if they have any) will have atrophied or never truly developed at all. Helping them acquire key people skills and learning how to start a conversation and keep it going is crucial.

I also wanted to help Doris attain some insight into why she was so reluctant to reach out to people. After a great deal of prompting (not an easy process), Doris became more prepared to say something about her background. I learned that she had had a very difficult childhood. She was an orphan, and had lived in an orphanage for many years. Unlike most of us, she had never known warmth or emotional connections with the adults who were responsible for her. From what I understood, her only emotional connections had been with a few other children at the orphanage. These were also the only people she (very occasionally) socialized with. Otherwise, her life seemed to be very lonely, apart from taking care of her two dogs. Doris had no close friends. She even rationalized why she had no need of friends, saying she was very happy as things stood. She never mentioned any romantic involvement. Clearly Doris had chosen a reclusive lifestyle, as she didn't feel confident or secure around others, behavior that was now negatively affecting her job. When she had been in a junior position, she had stayed under the radar, but that was no longer the case.

When coaching people like Doris, you need to tread very carefully, as they are very easily spooked. And don't be fooled by their manner. They may appear not to care about what's going on around them or about their relationship with you as coach, but the reality is very different. While they may seem aloof, some of them (not the dismissive-avoidant type) may actually feel extremely emotionally sensitive and lonely. They would like to come closer but are scared to do so, given their previous painful experiences. They need a lot of personal space and a considerable amount of time before they are ready to open up about their inner life. Although I needed to reach out to Doris, I always reminded myself not to push too hard and scare her.

In any form of executive coaching, gaining and keeping the client's trust is essential. With people with attachment disorders, developing a rapport and a trusting coaching relationship will be a slow, gradual process that may never fully develop. As a coach you will have to work to ensure your client's security in the coaching relationship. Acknowledging the client's boundaries will be more important than it might be in other coaching situations, and you will need to be on your guard not to confront your client on this kind of issue. I needed to be careful not to "smother" Doris and to tolerate some possible "acting-out" behaviors.

I felt it was important to understand something of the psychodynamics of Doris's early history. Emotional recovery from past experiences of grief and loss is going to be key in almost all types of attachment intervention. Doris and I spent a considerable amount of time on these issues. It turned out that both her parents had died in a car accident and that no other family member had been willing to take her on—an excellent prescription for feeling unwanted. As she became more trusting of me, she opened up to talk about her anger, sadness, and loneliness during the many years she spent at the orphanage. I felt that these explorations provided her with some insight into the origin of her feelings, and her behavior pattern of distancing herself from people. I also devoted a lot of energy to helping Doris improve her general coping skills and become better at social interaction and communication. These improvements—and the small successes she scored—proved to be quite helpful in boosting her sense of self-esteem.

After our 12 sessions were up, I suggested that Doris could still continue to see me if she wanted and I also suggested that she might enter a group therapy program. I hoped that being in a group setting, where she would have an opportunity to interact with others, would help Doris practice and improve her new interpersonal skills. This was something I could not have suggested earlier in our relationship. The idea would have been too frightening for her and she would probably have clammed up disastrously. Alternatively, if she had joined a group too soon, she might have quit prematurely, unable to tolerate being part of a social group. But after all the preliminary work we had done, I felt confident that Doris would be able to handle a group situation. She had worked hard on improving her sense of self and had acquired the minimal social skills and abilities to tolerate group dynamics much better. I felt that the group sessions would add to the support structure she needed, and increase her social motivation.

I saw Doris off and on for another year. I was very pleased to see how she was developing. The last time I saw her, she told me that she had gone "beyond her dogs"—and described that she had entered into a serious relationship. Also, although I knew that things were much better at work, it was nice to have it confirmed by my colleague, who expressed her satisfaction at how well Doris was doing. She told me that they had even given her back her original portfolio.

chapter **4**

The Paranoid Executive

In this world only the paranoid survive.

—*Dean Koontz*

Just because you're paranoid doesn't mean they aren't after you.

—*Joseph Heller*

People that have trust issues only need to look in the mirror. There they will meet the one person that will betray them the most.

—*Shannon L. Alder*

Henry Kissinger once said, "Even a paranoid can have enemies." This is very true, and paranoid types will present you with some of your more difficult coaching assignments. That doesn't negate the fact that healthy suspicion can be viewed as an adaptive mechanism. Being vigilant for real or potential obstacles can be seen as an extension of anybody's natural wish to survive. But suspiciousness needs to be moderated by a healthy dose of reality in case it slips over into full-fledged paranoia. Effective executives ground their behavior in sound organizational practices that limit and test danger, and they rely on trusted associates to help them stay sound and sane. The truly suspicious types, however, look at these matters quite differently.

Be prepared to accept that it's fairly normal for all of us to have some degree of paranoia about the situations we will encounter in our lives (such as worry about an impending set of layoffs at work). However, really suspicious people take this to an extreme. Their paranoia pervades virtually every professional and personal relationship they have. They can't distinguish between danger and security, so they see danger everywhere and hostile intent in everyone. Typically, they question the trustworthiness of people around them, and can suffer from delusions of conspiracy and victimization. And this is what makes paranoid people so troublesome.

Earlier, I called paranoia the "disease of kings." Persecutory paranoia and paranoid grandiosity are common in power and politics. Premier league players include Caligula, Tamerlane, Ivan the Terrible, Adolf Hitler, Joseph Stalin, Pol Pot, Kim Il-Sung, Saddam Hussein, and Robert Mugabe.

Truly paranoid individuals distort information and engage in delusional thinking and faulty reality testing. Always bear in mind that in trying to deal with perceived dangers, they create what seems to them a logical world—acute dangers require drastic measures, after all. However, while their reasoning may be rational, the assumptions on which their logic is based are false. In other words, you can look at paranoid behavior as a form of rationality run amok.

For paranoid types, it's a harsh world, empty of compromise. Given their inner insecurities (always feeling threatened), they must constantly wage war with external enemies. They are skilled at externalizing their inner fears. Believing that all bad things come from the outside and all good things from within, they cannot accept that some of the bad things that happen to them are a consequence of their own doing. They look for others to blame—and punish—for any setbacks they experience. By creating a stark bipolar world of enemies and friends they introduce a modicum of certainty into an otherwise unpredictable world. As you can imagine, with friends and enemies clearly differentiated, choices can be made without hesitation.

Thus paranoia is both the disease of kings and its cause. Fearing that others may do them harm, they look for, and find, hidden meanings in even the most innocent remarks. Suspicious types are prone to believe that other people's motives are suspect or even malevolent. If, after a cursory check, their suspicion seems unjustified, rather than feeling relief paranoids will look ever deeper for confirmation.

Keep in mind that your paranoid clients will resort to rather primitive defense mechanisms in stressful situations. All of us are capable of "splitting" (dividing people into "good" and "bad") or projecting our problems onto others, which may once have been adaptive defense mechanisms; with paranoids they become maladaptive. Paranoid types never seem to progress beyond a world of extreme images of good and evil, enemies and friends; they seem to be incapable of understanding that the same person can trigger both good and bad feelings.

When coaching these people, always remember that they fear being exploited, harmed, or deceived, even where there's no evidence that this might happen. They may interpret your innocent actions as ploys to damage them. Minor slights can quickly arouse major hostility, with bad feelings persisting for a long time. As you might imagine, their combative and suspicious nature may elicit hostile responses from others, which then serve to confirm their original expectations. Unsurprisingly, paranoids are adept at self-fulfilling prophecies. The extent to which they will go in questioning others' loyalty and trustworthiness can be scary, as can the degree to which they bear grudges and their unforgiving attitude to perceived insults, injuries, or slights. Paranoids are masters of litigiousness.

The *modus operandi* of suspicious people causes serious relationship problems and interferes with their ability to function socially and at work. These people are not easy to get along with. And as clients, they will not endear themselves to you: their excessive suspiciousness may be expressed as argumentativeness, recurrent complaining, or hostile aloofness. Also, because they are hyper-vigilant for potential threats, they be guarded, secretive, or devious and appear "cold" and lacking in softer feelings.

I hope for your sake that you will not have many clients who fit this bill. Not only will they provide you with little opportunity for coaching success, but they can also make your life miserable. As trust management is an essential factor in coaching, dealing with them can be a true challenge. Their distrust of others, including you as a coach, will make your coaching assignment extraordinarily difficult. Despite your best efforts, they will always read hidden critical or threatening meaning into any comment you make.

Another difficulty in dealing with paranoid types is that they are highly unlikely to seek out help themselves. The most likely scenario is that others will ask you to help them. Paranoids only look for coaching when their problems start to impact significantly on their lives, or following some kind of traumatic event that becomes a catalyst for their need for help.

The exact cause of paranoia is not really known, but it is likely to involve a combination of biological, genetic, social, and psychological factors. I have been struck, through personal observation, by the frequency with which early childhood experiences, including physical or emotional trauma, turn out to play an important role in the development of a paranoid outlook. And ominously, if people have this problem, they are quite likely to pass it on to their children.

Let me give you an example of a client who demonstrated this kind of behavior. Some time ago, one of my associates was doing a top-team group intervention. Its purpose was to make the members of the team work together more effectively. During the workshop, it became clear that one of the members (let's call him Don), although technically extremely talented, was a disaster from a managerial perspective. He had very poor interpersonal skills, was terrible at motivating people, and not a team player. The feedback he had received revealed that his inability to work with others was becoming a serious burden for the company. The CEO, who had been disturbed about Don's behavior for quite some time, was ready to get rid of him, but encouraged by his COO, was prepared to offer him a final chance. My associate was asked if she would take Don on as a client. Her response was that it was a bad idea, given that the CEO was an existing client, but that she would refer Don to someone else. And that was where I came in.

I knew from previous experience that dealing with someone like Don wasn't going to be an easy ride. The long-term prognosis for people with paranoid behavior patterns is not good. Early termination of a coaching arrangement is more usual than not. Every time you work with paranoid types, you run up against the trust issue.

But you may have an ally in your work. Some paranoids suffer from anxiety or depression, a sign that their defenses are not working properly, and it is exactly these feelings that may convince them that they need help. However, don't get your hopes up too much. You may be lucky, and some of them will respond positively to coaching, but I'm afraid that the majority will return to paranoid la-la land. The bottom line in working with these people is that if there's the slightest desire for change, the prospects for progress will be better. Generally, however, individuals who suffer from this dysfunctional outlook often remain afflicted with prominent symptoms of it throughout their lives.

As you know, creating a working alliance is a major part of any meaningful coaching relationship and provides the framework and the basis on which coaching work proceeds for all your clients. Building trust with people like Don is going to be much more difficult than it will be with other types of difficult executive.

To assure a trustful relationship, starting on day one you need to assure your paranoid client of the complete confidentiality of the work the two of you are going to do together. You must state upfront that you will have nothing to do with anybody else in the company and have no further communication with the individual responsible for the referral. You should also let the client know what information you received about him or her.

And that's exactly what I did with Don. I have learned the hard way to be very straightforward with suspicious clients. Apart from anything else, their sense of humor tends to be limited, so subtle jokes and references are often lost. In exchanges with people like Don, you need to be as matter of fact as possible. To preempt any surge of paranoia, I told Don at our first session all the information I had received from my associate. (Information about the client not received directly from the client's mouth will raise a great deal of suspicion.)

My first meeting with Don was in his office and it didn't get off to a good start. He was standoffish and although he gave an initial impression of being a highly rational and unemotional individual, I recognized an undertone of hostility, stubbornness, and sarcasm in the way he talked to me. But he also seemed depressed. In spite of his putting a positive spin on things, I think he knew that things weren't going the way they should.

Don said he was willing to spend some time with me, although he didn't really see the need. He felt that he had been victimized in the workshop. His impression was that the other members of the top team were all jockeying for the CEO's job, as the CEO had announced that he planned to retire in a few years' time. Don saw himself as a serious candidate and maintained that some of the other key members of the team had had it in for him for a long time. The workshop had brought matters to a head and they made him the scapegoat. However, he wanted to stay in the company and was willing to give coaching a try. Despite this positive stance, I could tell from the language he used that he was reluctant to confide in me because he feared that whatever information he gave me might be used against him maliciously.

When I asked Don gently if he could tell me a little bit more about the goings-on in the company, I received a venomous earful. Don certainly didn't hold back. According to him, the company had a Darwinian culture and working there was like swimming with sharks. People got into a lot of fights. It should be said that this was not the impression I had received from others—quite the reverse.

I was intrigued by his descriptions of these fights and the "people out to get him." It was a theme repeated again and again. Was it just bad luck or was Don the author of his own misery? My educated guess was the latter. The "out to get me" theme was also demonstrated in a number of litigations Don was involved in, usually concerning things he had bought from people who had been engaged in "fallacious advertising." Clearly, I was dealing with someone who bore deep grudges and neither forgot nor forgave any insult he imagined to have received. Although I felt somewhat brought down by his litany of complaints, the good news was that I didn't think Don's symptoms were psychotic, which can be the case with paranoid disturbances. He had sufficient grasp on reality for me to think that some progress might be possible.

As our discussions progressed, I learned that Don was divorced and that his wife had taken the initiative to end the marriage. I suspected—but I may be wrong—that she had become tired of his suspiciousness and his accusations that she was having an affair. My grounds for thinking so were Don's repeated derogatory remarks about the fidelity of spouses or partners. I got the impression that Don, like many other people with paranoid behavior patterns, was not only pathologically jealous, but also over-controlling and overly critical. Listening to the problems he'd encountered in his personal life, it was clear to me that his suspicious behavior had a negative impact way beyond his business activities. It was destroying his life.

When dealing with people like Don, you have to make your moves very carefully. Paranoids are not good collaborators. You must be prepared to encounter a lot of resistance. They will be hypersensitive to everything you say and highly critical of it. Remember that people like Don are likely to misunderstand any act of kindness or words of encouragement or misinterpret them as a cover for more malevolent intentions. They are quick to react angrily or to counterattack.

Another important thing to remember in dealing with people like Don is that their behavior may not bring out the best in you. Paranoia attracts paranoia. You will have to monitor yourself very carefully. Don't allow yourself to be driven mad. Keep your cool. Be prepared for any comment you make to be interpreted as an attack on your client's character or reputation—even so, your client's outbursts will often catch you completely unawares. That was very much how Don functioned. For a long time, he remained suspicious of my intentions, with no justification.

At the core of paranoids' mindset are feelings of inadequacy. Starting in childhood, their feelings of impotence taught them always to be on guard and prepared to lash out. To change his behavior patterns, I needed to enhance Don's sense of adequacy and self-efficacy. I needed to engage in a confidence-building process. A part of this would be reworking his many cognitive distortions, particularly his tendency to blame others. Part of this process involved helping him improve his interpersonal skills. Basically, I needed to help Don put a stop to whatever vicious circles he was caught in.

And as if this challenge was not enough, I also had to accept that he would mistrust the coaching process, particularly in the early stages.

The key to working with paranoids is to try to keep things simple. Initially, the kind of coaching that emphasizes a simple supportive approach may be the most effective. In trying to create a working relationship with Don, I was using the technique of "collaborative empiricism," a form of cognitive coaching whereby Don and I would jointly examine his beliefs in the light of objective evidence. This proved useful. The specific themes we worked on included Don's belief that other people were always malicious and deceptive, and his need to be constantly on the lookout for threats. At the same time (when appropriate), I needed to accept (and acknowledge) the possibility that there might be a kernel of truth to Don's suspicions, knowing what I did about the power games in the company.

While simplicity was the key to this intervention, I didn't limit myself to a cognitive, supportive form of coaching. I also included a solid dose of psychodynamic understanding to provide Don with insights about the reasons he was behaving the way he did. I thought that this combination of interventions would be most effective, but I was careful not to overload him. I tried to pace whatever I thought he could tolerate. I knew that, in general, group interventions—like the workshop in which he had performed so badly—are always difficult for people like Don. Group coaching is not the intervention of choice for paranoids; it's doubtful whether the crucial trust issues can ever be dealt with sufficiently for them.

As the coaching progressed and Don became more trusting of me I had to be careful to balance my objective responses against his at times bizarre paranoid thoughts. This wasn't always easy, even after I had established a good rapport with him. During the times when he acted out his paranoid beliefs, I really needed to control myself. But I knew that if I challenged Don too closely I risked his cancelling our sessions.

Gradually, Don also came to understand that his negative childhood experiences—the threatening atmosphere at home, where he never knew when his stepfather would lash out at him—had contributed to his paranoid mindset. It seemed his mother hadn't been much help. The few times he had confided in her, she had betrayed him to his stepfather. These conversations gave him deeper insight into why he behaved the way he did, why he was always on his guard and needed to lash out. These reflections helped him to identify and understand what underpinned his dysfunctional core beliefs.

As time went on, I became more and more successful at challenging Don's negative beliefs and thought processes, and replacing them with more positive and true ones. And there were signs of progress: Don became more directly and immediately in touch with his feelings of vulnerability, inferiority, and weaknesses; he became better at controlling his frequently overwhelming and confusing feelings; and he came to understand his sense of victimhood. Don was working on changing some of his core beliefs. I was making inroads. I think an important factor was that I was able to show empathy with, tolerance for, and nonjudgmental acceptance of the material Don brought to the coaching sessions, an attitude he very much appreciated.

Fortunately, I wasn't alone in helping Don experiment with different ways of dealing with people. Midway in our journey, he found a soulmate within the company. This rather straight-talking woman helped him to redirect his energies in a more playful manner. (Fun was not the first thing that came to mind with Don.) Thanks to his girlfriend, he began to build more of a life outside work. She eventually advised Don to leave the company and find an opportunity elsewhere, where he didn't have a history.

After he left the company, Don continued seeing me for some time as a private client. Six months after he had quit his job (and was working elsewhere), he thanked me for my work, saying that he thought that he could now manage on his own. He felt that his new job and his girlfriend had given him enough stability to face the future. I wished him all the best, and I haven't seen him since.

Do you think this was a successful coaching intervention? I thought it was. True, the company had made an investment in Don and lost him. However, I believe what happened was for the best for both parties. Don made a new beginning, while the company did what was right and gave a talented but troubled individual another chance.

5

The "Bipolar" Executive

Insanity is relative. It depends on who has who locked in what cage.

—*Ray Bradbury*

When you are mad, mad like this, you don't know it. Reality is what you see. When what you see shifts, departing from anyone else's reality, it's still reality to you.

—*Marya Hornbacher*

There comes a time when the blankness of the future is just so extreme, it's like such a black wall of nothingness. Not of bad things like a cave full of monsters and so, you're afraid of entering it. It's just nothingness, the void, emptiness and it is just horrible. It's like contemplating a future-less future and so you just want to step out of it. The monstrosity of being alive overwhelms you.

—*Stephen Fry*

Cyclothymia is a mild form of bipolar disorder characterized by mood swings. Cyclothymics can feel on top of the world for a period of time, followed by a period when they feel low. In between times they can be stable and well. Their emotional ups and downs are not as extreme as those of people who suffer from full-fledged manic depression, whose mood swings can be much more devastating and long-lasting. However, this doesn't mean that cyclothymic behavior has no consequences. This leadership style can end in career derailment, job loss, estrangement from friends and family members, major financial problems, drug abuse, alcoholism, hospitalization, and even suicide attempts. There is generally less awareness of cyclothymia than of the more dramatic bipolar disorder.

While cyclothymics in a depressive state have little energy, the opposite is true when they are in a hypomanic state, barely sleeping and feeling euphoric. In this mode, they can be extremely energetic, flamboyant, and expansive. When they are up, they think positively and remain defiantly optimistic in the face of adversity. They assume risks easily and make bold moves. They are on a mission to find stimulation, novelty, and excitement. They make impressive efforts to make their dreams come true. In an organizational context, hypomanic executives can achieve a great deal in terms of building, revitalizing, and transforming organizations and taking others with them on their quest for adventure.

However, there is also the other side to the cycle. Depression is always around the corner.

One day I had a call from an old client, asking for advice. He was at his wits' end trying to "manage" his CEO (let's call him Frank). He said something along the lines of, "Wouldn't it be nice if all the people you worked with were well-balanced and happy? Wouldn't life be simpler if you knew what to expect from their emotional state?"

Unfortunately, life is rarely that utopian. Although high highs and low lows are uncommon at senior executive level—the emotional register of most falls in a middle range—there are exceptions, and Frank was clearly one of them. Frank's behavior could be very puzzling and disturbing, and seemed to operate at the extremes of the emotional spectrum. My old client told me that Frank seemed to have no emotional middle ground; he said working with Frank had turned him into a firefighter—running behind him and putting out the emotional blaze Frank left in his wake. Frank's emotional and behavioral volatility was starting to affect the firm. But the situation wasn't that straightforward. My old client said that Frank's energy and ebullience could be contagious. At times he had an enormous amount of energy that he directed to the people who worked for him. And he had a knack of drawing people to him, which had indisputably contributed to the original success of the firm.

As I listened, I started to picture Frank as the Pied Piper, a charismatic leader who entranced those around him while leading them to their doom. When I said this to my old client, he said that was exactly right: the firm seemed to be on hold, with a failed expansion, a looming liquidity problem, and a disquietingly high turnover of capable executives. Although it sounded like "mission impossible," I was intrigued. It would be an interesting challenge. I promised to visit the head office and meet Frank.

Cyclothymic people have probably had mood swing problems for as long as they can remember. This was certainly the case with Frank. When we met, he told me that there had been several periods in his life when he had been wildly out of control, dominated by soaring highs and melancholy lows. He revealed that some years before his wife had become increasingly worried about his unstable behavior and that he had consulted a psychiatrist who had prescribed medication. Lithium had helped him for a while, but it had been a mixed experience. Life on lithium was flat, less exciting. Frank felt it led to a dampening of his emotional experiences and he didn't like the side effects. He missed the "high highs," so had stopped taking the drug. He would rather have occasional states of euphoria and depression than the middle-of-the-road state he experienced on medication.

When you deal with people like Frank, you need to make an effort to get under their skin and understand what it means to feel "high." While on a "high," a simple thing like, for example, walking in the park, can become an almost mystical experience. The way Frank described it to me, with his senses fully operating his awareness of all the objects in his environment would be intensified. Whatever he did—looking at the garden, listening to birds, talking to an associate, making a deal—he experienced much more deeply. Frank was clearly addicted to his highs. He said he believed they benefited his work as well. They increased his productivity and that of the people around him. His hypomanic mood energized his colleagues and helped them actualize the projects in which they were involved. But when the euphoria left, life had a dead and deadening quality.

While in an elevated mood state, people like Frank tend to undertake extremely risky ventures, stimulated by their own expansiveness, often unwarranted optimism, impulsiveness and poor judgment. Caught up in their grandiosity, they overestimate their capabilities and take on more than they can handle—more, indeed, than anyone could. In Frank's case, the problem was aggravated by his inclination to deny that his behavior was problematic. The people around him reckoned that he realized, at least subliminally, that his cyclothymic behavior was causing problems; however, he resisted all offers of help. And because he could put on a good façade, until very recently he had been able to convince others that there was nothing the matter.

Listening to Frank, I learned that his marriage, when he was 23, had helped to balance his moods to some degree. His wife had brought a modicum of stability to his life. Recently, however, as their children became more independent, she had embarked on a part-time career and was less available to him. This had changed the equilibrium in the home, as they saw less and less of each other. With his wife preoccupied with professional concerns, Frank began to spend even more time at the office and away on travel.

When I got to know Frank better, he reluctantly confessed (when asked) that he had had a number of affairs. He wasn't sure whether his wife knew about them, but it was clear to him that his behavior had affected their relationship. According to Frank, he and his wife were like ships that passed in the night. When prompted further, he admitted that he longed for their previous intimacy—or, as he said smilingly, he would like the ships to meet more often.

From our conversations, I also learned that Frank was no stranger to substance abuse. He often turned to alcohol when he was feeling high, because alcohol seemed to prolong and intensify the euphoria. He denied being an alcoholic, but admitted that he drank a few whiskeys every day. He had also experimented with drugs, particularly cocaine.

To me, the million-dollar question was what could be done to stabilize Frank's behavior, and in doing so, revitalize the firm. The situation had become critical. The other key executives in the firm had told me that the present situation couldn't go on much longer. Frank's erratic behavior had traumatized people and too many high-quality people had left—a costly loss. If Frank's behavior couldn't be contained in one way or another, the firm could get into real problems.

For people suffering from a serious manic-depressive disorder, the treatment of choice is psychotherapy in combination with medication. It seemed likely to me that Frank's milder cyclothymia might be helped by medication that would free him from the devastation caused by his depressive and manic episodes. Psychotherapy could also help him understand the psychological implications of his mood swings and their effects, and persuade him of the need to take medication to prevent a recurrence.

But suggesting is one thing: cyclothymics (and Frank was no exception) are rarely receptive to such advice. While "high" they rarely have insight into their condition. Their reality testing is often impaired: whether high or low, they may not have a sense of how they are perceived by and treat others. Denial is a frequent defense mechanism among cyclothymics, a form of resistance that seriously impairs their critical faculties. In a hypomanic state they are reluctant to admit that their behavior is unacceptable.

As in every coaching relationship, the way to deal with people like Frank is to build trust. In some cases, it can also be useful to cross boundaries and talk to a client's spouse or partner. And that's what I did with Frank. First, I had a very fruitful conversation with Frank's wife alone, and later a few times together with Frank. It was important to understand her thinking: how she dealt with her husband, how she saw the future, and whether the future included both of them.

After I had developed a working alliance with both Frank and his wife, I began to explore with Frank various scenarios about how he saw himself in the future. What did he really want? Where would he like to be? Who were the people who would be part of his future?

Once Frank realized how important his relationships with his wife and children were, he had an incentive to do something about his situation. When we discussed his future in the company, reflecting on his strengths, it dawned on Frank that he needed to play a different role. He had a strong tendency toward micro-management, but becoming involved in detail made him overexcited, often in a negative way. As our coaching sessions progressed, he came to the decision to appoint a COO who would take care of a lot of that aspect of running the business. Frank realized that his greatest contribution derived from his contacts with important clients and that that was where he should direct his energy.

During a transitional period like this, your role as an executive coach may become less well defined; you might find yourself more consultant than coach, and you may also find that you have to cross more boundaries. In Frank's case, I held several discussions with members of his executive team on how to structure the company in a way that would be acceptable to Frank. I also talked to a number of non-executive directors—I felt it was necessary to get buy-in from all the stakeholders. A kind of organizational architecture was devised that would take advantage of Frank's remarkable talents while neutralizing the darker side of his behavior. Over a period of six months I managed to coach Frank so that he was left with the structure he needed to stabilize his mental state, both at home and at work. I also introduced him to a psychotherapist whom he saw at least once a week for some time to follow.

6

The Psychopathic Executive

Your greatest enemy will hide in the last place you would ever look.

—*Julius Caesar*

It takes many sheep to satisfy one wolf.

—*Nenia Campbell*

[Classically,] true psychopaths were not successful. For the most part, they were major screw-ups.

—*Chris Patrick*

Imagine what it would be like to be completely free of internal restraints, and able to do whatever you feel like doing. Imagine having no conscience and no feelings of remorse or guilt, no matter what nasty things you might do. Imagine a world in which you care only about yourself, about fulfilling your own needs, and have absolutely no concern for the well-being of others. Imagine having no sense of responsibility toward others, and giving no thought to the shameful, harmful, or immoral actions that you might take.

I'm asking you to imagine a total emotional deficit. Wouldn't it be a blessing in some ways? Wouldn't life be so much simpler and more pleasurable without inhibitions, moral conscience or a sense of responsibility toward others?

Having a conscience is a nuisance; empathy's a drag. Without the pangs of shame and guilt, you could do anything—nothing would hold you back.

Difficult, isn't it? Most of us assume that a conscience is a universal human feature, so it's hard to imagine not having one. And because of that, the people who do function without one, with the exception of the occasional historical tyrant or dictator, are to all intents and purposes invisible to us. We don't recognize them, and we are certainly unprepared to deal with them in our daily lives.

Nevertheless, we have to accept that a small portion of the population has a psychological makeup and mindset very different from the rest of us. Although they have within themselves great dysfunctionality and destructiveness, they can also blend in and assume a kind of stealth position within organizations and society. Indeed, these people may not even realize that they *are* different. Unaware of the effect of their behavior on others, they are blind to their own shortcomings. And their lack of conscience means that the usual tools for societal regulation are irrelevant and don't work. What's more, the implications of this kind of behavior can be severe. Such people, who are often described as psychopaths, can bring havoc to the lives of others. This doesn't mean that all tough and demanding bosses fall into this category. Demanding bosses are OK as long as they are respectful and fair, and their primary motivation is to obtain the best from the people who work for them.

Psychopaths have always been around. Many historical figures who committed crimes against humanity fall within this category. All of us know that in situations of war, poverty, economic breakdown, epidemic, or political strife, for example, psychopaths can acquire the status of saviors. We only have to think of Adolf Hitler, Joseph Stalin, Mao Zedong, Kim Jong-Il, Saddam Hussein, Serbia's Slobodan Milosevic and Radovan Karadzic, or Syria's Bashar al-Assad, for some real-life examples. And we often come across psychopaths in popular fiction and films—watching television series about serial killers seems to be a regular pastime. These morally depraved individuals represent the "monsters" in our society, inevitable and incorrigible predators whose crimes are calculated and emotionless.

Happily, only a small subset of psychopaths become the violent criminals fictionalized in films and novels. But there are many less extreme forms of psychopathy quite different from those associated with the kind of character disorder found among the criminal types. Not all psychopaths are destined for prison; some may even be in top executive positions. Indeed, wherever power, control, status, and money are at stake, such individuals abound. The games that typify a considerable part of organizational life come naturally to them. Unlike the monstrous historical figures mentioned above, they are not blatantly violent or antisocial. Instead, they channel their energies in less obvious, less violent ways. They know how to conceal their malevolence in order to manipulate others to their ends.

If I were to construct a spectrum of pathology, "heavy" psychopaths, both fictional and historical, would weigh down one end, while successful psychopathic "lite" executives would be at the other. Unlike fundamental psychopaths, born without the capacity to form emotional bonds (due to possible genetic abnormalities), "lite" psychopaths experience a deactivation of the development of basic affective patterns (due to the interplay of nature–nurture). In their case, we can assume that developmental forces have played a more significant role. Their empathic responses may have been incapacitated due to repeated disillusionment in childhood, caused by physical or sexual abuse or other forms of mistreatment. Over time, these negative environmental experiences have led to the deactivation or poor development of neurological pathways, resulting in psychopathic behavior patterns. Later in life, affective inhibition can have serious consequences, particularly if psychopaths function on a larger stage—within organizations or society.

My term for these "lite" psychopaths is *seductive operational bullies*— SOBs—in this case not the kind of person usually associated with that particular acronym. Compared to "heavy" psychopaths, most of whom can be found in prisons or mental hospitals, SOBs are better at creating a consistent guise of normality. Indeed, their behavior may even be so well matched to certain organizations that they reach the top.

I have found that SOBs can be quite effective, at least for a while. Many global corporations are highly attractive to people who are eager to advance themselves at the expense of others and the companies they work for and are unburdened by conscience. Financial institutions in particular tend to be playing fields on which SOB executives thrive. Because such institutions require a high level of trust in order to function effectively, we often wrongly assume that the people who run them are honorable. But SOB executives, of whom trustworthiness is not a feature, flock to them. They feed on the trust placed in them by others to their own advantage—and such feeding is frequently pathological in nature.

Although their stealth makes them hard to recognize, there are plenty of SOB executives out there and they are more common at the higher levels of organizations than in the general population. So there's a fair chance of having a pathological boss. Unfortunately, most people lack the knowledge and skills to effectively identify, respond, and deal with SOBs. Either they don't understand the cause of their problems or they don't know how to fight back. And to make matters worse, SOB executives usually have the dedication, focus, and business acumen to create the appearance of success.

The weapons they use include emotional blackmail, dishonest yet persuasive language, discrediting others around them, deflecting the issue at hand when confronted, concealed threats, and lies or distortion of the facts. They have mastered the art of manipulation disguised as helpfulness, good intentions, and working "for the good of the company." They are very talented at hiding their true motives while making others look incompetent, uncooperative, or self-serving. They are skilled at making others lose their jobs, getting others to do their job for them, and even getting others to apologize for confronting them about their manipulative behavior. The only thing that counts for SOBs is winning. Winning means getting their way and maintaining a position of power and control over others.

They also know how to make others emotionally dependent on them. They prey on their emotional vulnerabilities. In particular, they are very skilled at winning over the boss, for example, by taking an interest in their family and hobbies, sharing their vices, offering to do their dirty work, and promising results if they are given free rein. They know how to undermine their opponents with subtle innuendo, making sure the slander reaches the major power-holders in the organization.

As they are extremely artful in their deception, most of us are oblivious to their underhand methods. Ironically enough, they are often held up as examples of leaders on the fast track. Masters at presenting an outward image of the good corporate citizen, they know how to play organizational power games. But while they are being rewarded for undeserved successes, frustration builds up among the people in their immediate entourage due to their intimidating, backstabbing, and manipulative ways. For people at their mercy, life in the organization can turn into a nightmare.

SOB executives are difficult to spot initially. Often, you will fail to recognize their Machiavellian disposition, and may even deny or rationalize their improper, unethical behavior. It doesn't help that people who are in the know are reluctant to admit that they have been betrayed or duped. The difficulty of convincing others of their manipulative behavior is compounded by their talent for making friends in high places who can protect them. For senior management, identifying and neutralizing SOBs requires the ability to pick up subtle signals in the organization. I'm sorry to say that not many have that skill.

Let me give you an illustration of a psychopathic executive. I had an email from Rosebeth, a regular client who was the CEO of a large consumer product company. Rosebeth was worried about Arnold, one of her high potentials who seemed to have a knack for rubbing a number of people up the wrong way. She had told him that unless he shaped up, there was no long-term future for him in the firm. To improve his "brand" of leadership she had advised him to work with an executive coach. As I had had a long-term relationship with Rosebeth, she had suggested my name to him, and Arnold seemed receptive to the idea.

I began by meeting Rosebeth to discuss her concerns about Arnold's behavior. I had a lot to hear. One of Rosebeth's main gripes was Arnold's tendency to blame others when things went wrong: "He remembers everyone's mistakes except his own. He's always in denial. It's like he has a selective memory." She added that other people on her team didn't really trust him. They told her that he broke his promises and breached confidences.

Rosebeth also talked about Arnold's over-competitiveness; it wasn't enough for him to succeed: others had to fail. Finally, he was a soloist rather than a team player, which ran counter to corporate culture. But to give him his due, Rosebeth said Arnold was smart, had great potential, and was charming to boot. In spite of advice she'd had to the contrary, she wanted to give him another chance.

As you might imagine, I was rather reluctant to take on the challenge. Would I be able to handle someone like Arnold? Could I really hope to make a difference?

On meeting Arnold for the first time, he gave the impression of being really on the ball. He was good-looking, gregarious, and very good at sweet-talking me. He had obviously Googled me beforehand and knew quite a bit about me. But his rather deferential manner didn't sit well with me. What was my intuition telling me? What was he trying to do with me? Whatever it was, it made me reluctant to ask the kind of pertinent questions that could help me pin down what Arnold was all about.

Rosebeth had given me a short overview of what some of the main issues were, so I put my concerns to one side and started by suggesting that Arnold undertake a 360-degree multi-party feedback exercise (or better still a 720-degree exercise that would include family members, friends, and people outside the work environment). Surprisingly, he seemed eager to oblige.

You will probably not be surprised to learn that when the results came back, they were incomplete. Feedback from a number of the important people with whom Arnold interacted (his subordinates in particular) was missing. It is usually the people who are unlucky enough to report to an SOB who are the first to recognize their dysfunctionality. SOBs take a very different approach to senior people in power. I decided not to let Arnold get away with it. I called him and asked him to do something about the missing results, making a point of naming the people he should include, which he grudgingly did.

As expected, the second report corroborated Rosebeth's comments and set the stage for a number of face-to-face coaching sessions. A number of Arnold's subordinates said that working for him could be very intimidating. He would lose it at times, which was bad enough, but what really upset them—and corroborated what Rosebeth had told me—was Arnold's tendency to take the credit for their work. Some also complained about his unpredictability and said that dealing with him was like walking on eggshells; you never knew what was going to hit you or when. Arnold had many interchangeable faces and could be charming one day, only to undermine you the next. So many of his promises turned out to be empty that some even accused him of being a habitual liar. He could seem honest and candid to your face, only to stab you in the back as soon as you turned away. One respondent made an unsubtle comment about Arnold's tendency toward sexual manipulation, hinting that he'd been involved in a number of office affairs.

The feedback also described Arnold's impression management skills and his habit of telling people what they wanted to hear. This made him remarkably effective in dealing with people he wanted to influence. I knew I would be one of them and I was sure that he would try do the same with me. From that perspective, I went into the coaching with my eyes open.

I thought it would be wise to let Arnold make his own interpretation of the feedback he had received, so I began by asking him how he had experienced it. What surprised him? What was fair? What was unfair? With people like Arnold, who react defensively, you have to play psychological judo. To gain leverage you have to avoid arguments and head-to-head confrontations. The first thing I had to do was to establish a working alliance to make our relationship effective.

As a general theme, I decided to work on ways to make Arnold happier in both his work and private life, neither of which seemed to me to be happy at that time. To achieve this, it helps to discuss possible discrepancies between the client's current behavior and the kind of future the client wants. Bringing these out into the open may ultimately create the motivation to change. In Arnold's case, I explored his ambitions for the future, explaining that his usual mode of interacting with people, which may have been effective at an earlier stage in his life, was ineffective in his current situation. I wanted to push him to make him see that something needed to change if he wanted to stay in the company and to be successful in his job.

People like Arnold can be formidable adversaries. You always have to be on guard against their manipulative side. There were times when I was at my wits' end with Arnold, as we made only pseudo-progress. Arnold was like an illusionist, trying out change mirages on me. Eventually, our sessions appeared to have modest results, as Rosebeth enthusiastically told me when I ran into her at a conference. She also mentioned that his colleagues appreciated the progress he was making and were more willing to give him the benefit of the doubt. I seemed to have "touched" Arnold.

But I was doubtful. Was there any true authenticity in Arnold's behavior? Had he really changed? I was not so sure. Although he had ostensibly made progress, I kept asking myself whether he was simply going through the motions, making an effort to toe the line only to further his ambitions.

Because of this, when I had a phone call from Rosebeth some time later asking me how I thought Arnold was doing, I wasn't sure what to say. I should say at this point that as a general rule I am non-committal (or preferably refuse to respond) when people in the organization where my client works ask me that question—after all Arnold was my client, not Rosebeth. But I genuinely didn't know what to say. I told Rosebeth that she would be the best judge of Arnold's progress as she worked closely with him. Her response was that she was very pleased, so much so that she planned to send Arnold to Southeast Asia to spearhead the company's expansion in that region. Don't be in such a rush, I cautioned. It might be better to keep Arnold close to head office, where there would be more control over his actions.

I was disappointed that my advice wasn't taken, but then again, I was probably insufficiently assertive. In due course, Arnold was sent to Asia. A year later, I read an article in the financial press about how Rosebeth's company had been involved in a major bribery scandal. The senior executive in that region (Arnold) had initiated a kickback operation of which he was one of the major beneficiaries. Apart from the company having to pay a substantial fine, the incident had sullied its reputation. Arnold was fired and given a suspended jail sentence.

When SOB executives seek treatment it is usually because it's a requirement imposed by their organization or because their continual posturing has exhausted them. I have learned from my experience working with SOB executives that their relationship with you, as an executive coach, will take one of two forms. Either they will try to enlist you as an ally against the people who "forced" them to undergo the exercise, or they will try to impress you to gain some other kind of advantage, generally of a legal nature. If you're wondering why I emphasize this point, and surprised by its specificity, I do so simply to put you on your guard for the pseudo-quality of what may look like miraculous improvements.

Finding yourself manipulated into either of these relationships with an SOB will be exasperating and frustrating. They always find new excuses for their behavior and new insights into others' vulnerabilities. More disturbingly, your intervention may actually help them to become more effective at manipulating people. For example, I remember one SOB who became an avid reader of therapeutic/coaching literature, acquiring the terminology to rationalize why he was doing what he was doing. Some will "mirror" what you want them to be and claim that they have seen the error of their ways. Others will express remorse for what they have done, but their words or actions will continue to contradict their contrition. And in the rare instances when executive coaching seems to have some effect, it doesn't take much for them to turn against you, the person who is trying to help them. Whatever working alliance is established, it will always remain very fragile.

One final, important point—you should be aware that SOB-like behavior in organizations is not limited to the incidental bad behavior of one individual. Organizations characterized by an organizational culture that encourages inappropriate behaviors and attitudes are not rare. In these organizations, unethical ways of doing things are condoned and even perpetuated by senior management. In such environments, executives may even view SOB-like behavior as normal or acceptable. SOB executives thrive when others in the organization condone or tolerate their behavior. You should view it as a vicious cycle, whereby the SOB, the victims, and the bystanders all play a role in creating these toxic power dynamics.

chapter **7**

The "Autistic" Executive

If your emotional abilities aren't in hand, if you don't have self-awareness, if you are not able to manage your distressing emotions, if you can't have empathy and have effective relationships, then no matter how smart you are, you are not going to get very far.

—*Daniel Goleman*

I've had it with you and your emotional constipation!
—*Washington Irving*

I don't have anything against my mom, but my family has no emotional connection to each other.
—*Adam Carolla*

The first five examples I have written about are dysfunctional types who can be difficult, but also quite charismatic. They don't leave you emotionally untouched. But some executives present a very different profile: for them it is their lack of emotional reactiveness, rather than an excess of it, that gives rise to problems.

In your work as a coach you will encounter clients who are unable to relate in depth to others, evidencing instead a state of emotional detachment that extends beyond relationships to every area of life. They have no feelings of zest, enthusiasm, or passion; their emotions are flattened and they appear to experience very little, if any, pleasure. In the absence of emotions, they live in a world where formality and ritual predominate. When this detachment appears in the workplace (especially in someone with a senior executive position) it affects the morale, spontaneity, and productivity of everyone who works with them.

In psychiatry, the word alexithymic is applied to people who are more commonly called "dead fish"—individuals who either struggle or are unable to understand emotions or to perceive the subtleties of mood change. The term comes from the Greek meaning "no word for emotions." Alexithymia covers a cluster of characteristics, including an inability to describe feelings verbally, an impoverished fantasy life, and over-pragmatic, unimaginative thought content. It is based on a large body of consistent clinical and phenomenological observations of a number of easily recognized features grouped under one umbrella term. As a communication disorder, alexithymic behavior is not uncommon.

I have heard a number of explanations for why people act in this way—some physiological, some psychological. Physiologists see it as a deficit in the connection between the left and right hemispheres of the brain; something has gone very wrong with the wiring between these two parts. Psychologists point to individuals' early relationships with their primary caregivers, where the mother uses the child as a "drug" and is apparently out of touch with the child's emotional needs. Having never had the opportunity to do so, the child (and later adult) never learns to manage its emotions in a situation-appropriate manner.

Whatever its source, in alexithymic individuals the ability to differentiate and verbalize emotions has never developed. And this inability to recognize emotions in turn impedes the construction of the highly complex matrix of emotional signals on which we all rely for daily functioning, and without which emotions are experienced as dangerous, potentially uncontrollable forces.

I have observed how alexithymics ignore their own mental and physical distress signals. Their fantasy life is stunted. Unable to create their own symbolic representations, fantasies, or dreams, in order to work through mental conflict they tend to resort to external stimuli as a way of giving structure to their world. They often need others to tell them how they feel. Interpersonal interactions make them uncomfortable, as they don't know how to react. No wonder that many of them function better in jobs that are "thing" oriented.

When coaching alexithymics, be aware that for them abstractions, tasks, ideas, and inanimate objects are of overriding importance. Feelings are superfluous; systems and structures are what really count. Their attachment to outward procedures, rules, and regulations becomes a way of coping with the sterility of their inner world. Unfortunately, being so "thing" focused makes their contacts with others depersonalized and mechanical.

Many alexithymics find refuge in information technology-oriented businesses. A systems person operates in an automaton-like way, hanging on to fixed routines or zealously advocating abstractions, abolishing relationships with real people. Interaction with an iPad or laptop seems to replace human stimulation; dealing with real people is another matter altogether. You quickly discover that alexithymics have not learned to decode others' subtle interpersonal signals, a defect that may cost them dearly in organizational life.

This doesn't mean that alexithymics cannot be successful. In fact, they often are, particularly within large, bureaucratic organizations where playing safe, making the right noises, predictability, and relative inconspicuousness are rewarded. But in senior positions in today's networked organizations they provide entirely the wrong sort of role model for others, and they are not very stimulating people to work for. Their mechanical way of doing things is no prescription for excellence.

Indeed, executives in the grip of alexithymia can bring down their organizations. Since they don't exude the dynamism, inspiration or vision that a high-performing organization needs, it's hard for them to motivate others to make exceptional efforts or stimulate in them a passion for learning and further development. And because they have difficulty dealing with the unpredictable—they often do not handle discontinuous change very well—they may impede progress. Their emotional absence can put a negative stamp on an organization's culture, discouraging creativity and strategic innovation, and may contribute to a decline in organizational performance.

I recall one executive, whom I shall call Robert, who sent me an email asking to see me. He wanted to discuss his sense of "stuckness"—he felt that he was at a dead end in his organization. Until recently he had been quite successful, but this was no longer the case.

Robert's problems had started when he changed jobs. He wondered whether he had made a mistake. When I asked Robert about his new job, he said that its lack of structure made him uncomfortable. It wasn't clear to him what he was really expected to do; there was great fluidity in relationships and structures. Clearly, things were not going well.

The structure of Robert's previous job, a more technical function in a government post, had either disguised his alexithymic behavior or provided some form of "containment." His rather mechanical way of operating had been successful there. Now he was chief information officer in a private company, a position that required considerable interpersonal skills. Robert was also having difficulty integrating with the other members of the top executive team. Not knowing what to do about it, he had spoken to his colleague in HR, who suggested it would be a good idea to do something about his emotional intelligence. This was why Robert had wanted an appointment with me. Would he would benefit from having an executive coach?

I am an optimist where personal and behavioral change is concerned, so I responded positively. And here was Robert, at our first face-to-face meeting, looking rather dejected. I was immediately struck by the mechanical way in which he answered my open-ended questions—always completely matter of fact, with a total absence of any playfulness. To be honest, I found his naivety about interpersonal matters somewhat endearing. From the way Robert talked about friends and family members, I also inferred that he had difficulty forming intimate relationships. When I asked him how he saw his future, his imagined scenario was devoid of any emotional content. Predictably, Robert's fantasy life and emotional memory, as is the case with many alexithymics, seemed to be impaired. On the positive side, he appeared to be intelligent and eager to learn.

Robert had great difficulty answering questions about how he would handle challenging interpersonal situations. Not only did he find it hard to respond, he was indecisive. Many of the situations genuinely baffled him. But he did recognize the difficulties he experienced in being part of a social group, and that he would become anxious when among people he didn't know. When faced with the unexpected, any decisiveness he had came from directing my question back to me—how would I have handled a particular situation?

When I asked Robert how he felt under stress, he mentioned stomach pains, muscle tension, and headaches, but was unable to articulate his corresponding feelings. It is typical of alexithymics to feel physically unwell rather than recognizing that they are emotionally affected. It was clear that Robert didn't understand why his body acted the way it did; it was simply beyond him.

In a similar situation, you should resist the temptation to encourage alexithymics to commit themselves to medical intervention (physicians take note). Indeed, you should be highly alert to the risk that you could end up colluding in unnecessary surgical and medical interventions. Despite his physical symptoms, Robert had recently been given a clean bill of health by his doctor, who, obviously at her wits' end, had wanted to refer him to a psychiatrist or psychotherapist. But Robert had not gone for that option. I was his practitioner of choice.

Something else to be alert to when coaching alexithymics is the boredom they typically evoke, which may undermine your effectiveness. Alexithymics communicate non-symbolically and respond behaviorally, and are not the most engaging clients. Indeed, some coaches assume they are not suited for any kind of intervention. While there is no dedicated medication for this disorder, antidepressants can sometimes be beneficial because alexithymia is known to be correlated with low moods. At times, the use of drugs makes it easier for alexithymics to focus on their feelings and the interpretation of their inner experiences.

In Robert's case, I created a basic narrative out of his difficulties. I felt that his inability to recognize or react to emotions appropriately was a dormant area that should be tackled gradually. If I were too "pushy" I might scare him into a direction that would be too uncomfortable. As is required in dealing with all clients, I needed to build the fundamentals of a working alliance.

What works best for me when dealing with alexithymics is to begin by exploring and finding solutions to their immediate interpersonal problems. To build a relationship with Robert, I first needed to help him to become more effective in his work environment. If that went well, I planned to add a modest dose of insight-oriented coaching into the mix. Although at times you may get bored, since alexithymics tend to be monotonous, you need to provide a supportive and sympathetic listening presence.

As Robert was inclined to somaticize his emotions, I encouraged him to describe what was happening to him when the symptoms occurred. I also encouraged him to talk about the feelings that came with the physical discomfort—this, as I expected, didn't come easily to him. I needed to help Robert understand the role that somatic symptoms played in his life. In the context of his various narratives, I explored with him the crucial, subjectively touching and painful experiences that had remained "unmentalized"—not properly expressed in language and not incorporated into his personal narrative. As time went on, I pushed Robert to explore the bodily experiences of his distress. My aim was to help him develop a lucid narrative about them and encourage him to reflect on how his experiences of distress would fit within the chain of the events described.

Gradually, after a considerable number of coaching sessions, Robert began to recognize how his physical symptoms were linked to emotionally disturbing events in his life. Our discussions had an increasing depth of feeling—for Robert, this was a new form of interacting and a way of dealing with others that also would be beneficial in his work environment. My hope was that in the process of coaching, neural pathways would be revitalized between the cortex and deeper centers of emotion. Maybe that was too much to expect, but whatever was happening, my interactions with Robert grew on me as time went on. I no longer felt bored with him.

He had become more playful, less mechanical. And, important from the perspective of work, he felt more comfortable in his new environment.

As the case of Robert illustrates, alexithymics can discover the emotional potential hidden deep within them. Like the Tin Woodman in *The Wizard of Oz*, who discovered that he had had a heart all along, executives like Robert can learn how to deal with emotions and no longer be afraid of them. And when they succeed in doing so, the change in relating to others goes a long way toward inspiring and getting the best out of people, raising morale, and making the organization a more exciting place to work.

My approach in dealing with Robert ultimately met with some success, but there are other intervention techniques available to people who have difficulties with emotional expressiveness. For example, group and family therapy can be beneficial, where group members and spouses lend assistance as educators of emotions. Through this kind of intervention, alexithymics learn to recognize, tolerate, and verbalize the emotional spectrum. It gives them a chance to practice their capacity for reflective self-observation. Behavioral techniques such as biofeedback, relaxation training, autogenic training, guided imagery, and hypnosis may also be of some help. These techniques may give them a sense of control over stressful responses, increasing their awareness of the relationship between bodily sensations and environmental events.

chapter 8

The Passive-Aggressive Executive

I believe that present day civilized man suffers from insufficient discharge of his aggressive drive.

—Konrad Lorenz

Passive pleasure is no pleasure at all.

—Arthur Adamov

I'm not passive-aggressive. If something bothers me, I think about it, then I act on it. I express it.

—Anton Yelchin

The term "passive-aggressive" is used to describe a behavior pattern where negative feelings are expressed indirectly rather than directly. Generally speaking, when someone yells at you, you know all is not well—they are making their feelings quite clear. But passive-aggressives are much more subtle in expressing their anger. They are masters of covert abuse. There is a disconnect between what they say and what they do. Nothing they do is done directly. They use a form of non-verbal aggression that manifests itself in negative behavior. This kind of sugarcoated hostility becomes a destructive way of interacting—a way of getting back at you without your recognizing their underlying anger. Unsurprisingly, passive-aggressives are very difficult to deal with.

In the organizational context, passive-aggressive executives will seem to agree overtly when a request is made, but will covertly express their resentment at what is demanded from them by missing deadlines, showing up late for meetings, making excuses, or even working against the task they've been assigned. Their sabotage takes the form of procrastination, inefficiency, and forgetfulness. Deadlines are for everyone, but not for them. They have their own time schedule. Superficially compliant, polite, friendly, down-to-earth, kind, and well-meaning, below the surface things are very different. Because passive-aggressives are unable to express themselves directly when they feel upset, annoyed, irritated, or disappointed, they bottle up their feelings and become obstructive and sulky, or stonewall those around them.

This behavior probably originated as a survival strategy within a family where the honest, direct expression of feelings was forbidden or dangerous. Children brought up in families with these interpersonal dynamics quickly learn to repress and deny their feelings and use other channels to express their frustration. They never learn to express anger in a healthier way. Even though their passive-aggressive stance may arouse their parents' wrath, it's still a safer option than expressing their anger directly. And this *modus operandi* will continue into adult life; they will continue to stifle their anger and be outwardly accommodating but actually obstructive in an underhanded way.

In fact, their feelings may be so successfully repressed that they don't consciously realize that they are behaving obstructively—they may fail to recognize their own anger or resentment. So when others are upset by their behavior they will take offence, because to their mind whatever caused the irritation was nothing to do with them—it was someone else's fault. Passive-aggressives always feel they are treated unfairly and are innocent victims of other people's unreasonable expectations.

Because of this, passive-aggressives are genuinely dismayed when confronted with their behavior. They don't realize that they are driving other people crazy. They are totally unaware how irritating it can be to deal with someone who agrees to do something but then doesn't do it. Their lack of insight into their own feelings means that passive-aggressives always feel misunderstood. If they are challenged about their behavior, they feel they are being held to unreasonable standards.

A senior executive I had been working with for some time referred Mary to me. He said he thought she had a lot of potential, but somehow never delivered on her promise. He gave me details that suggested a variety of self-destructive behaviors; listening to him, I had the mental picture of someone determined to "snatch defeat out of the jaws of victory." After some back and forth—I wasn't that keen to take Mary on—I agreed to see her. From the senior executive's description, I realized that I might be dealing with someone with passive-aggressive characteristics, and from previous experience of working with people like Mary I knew she was unlikely to be insightful about her infuriating behavior. Passive-aggressives are usually unaware that their difficulties are of their own making. They rarely volunteer for coaching. And they are very resistant to change.

During our first face-to-face meeting, I experienced Mary as cold, passive, even rather depressed. When I asked her why she was seeing me, she could not give a coherent answer. The only thing she could come up with was that the person she worked for had told her that it would be a good idea. In spite of having gone through a 360-degree feedback exercise, she didn't seem to realize that other people were perturbed by her behavior. As I questioned her, it became clear that her view of the world was pessimistic and negative. She had few positive things to say about her life, either at home or at work. When I asked her about her co-workers and her boss, she said she often found them unreasonable. After our initial coaching session, I noted that Mary seemed to have little self-confidence.

It took some time to warm to Mary. Every coaching session left me feeling irritable. She was quick to acquiesce with everything I said, but even as she did so I felt a subtle, unspoken resentment at having to be with me. I started to wonder whether she had come to me voluntarily or whether she hadn't had a choice in the matter. I felt the latter was probably closer to the truth.

When I asked about her various relationships, Mary confessed that they were somewhat strained but couldn't explain why. Asking her about her work, I got the sense that she was angry with her boss, although she seemed to be unable to express it openly. I wasn't clear to me whether she felt that she herself played a role in the poor chemistry between the two of them.

I quickly realized that I'd need a "Teflon coating" to be able to deal with Mary. Passive-aggressive people often feel a sense of accomplishment when they know they have managed to irritate or frustrate you. And Mary clearly knew how to get my goat. I experienced very strong counter-transference reactions (the complex of feelings I had towards her) during our sessions. I knew I needed to stay calm and level-headed, and hold my emotions in check. I was able to control myself, but the effort not to let her get to me took a lot out of me.

Passive-aggressive individuals do not often keep their word or promise, which puts an additional strain on a coaching relationship, especially if you intend to give them "homework"—they're unlikely to do it despite assuring you that they will. But nevertheless, giving them homework can be helpful as it is a way of bringing their problems out into the open.

If Mary wanted to progress in her career, I needed to help her realize how her passive-aggressive behavior was affecting others negatively. She had to find better ways to control her anger and anxiety and to learn to express her feelings more directly. It was my task to help her to find more effective and satisfying coping strategies to deal with the stress she was experiencing at work and at home. Above all, Mary needed to resolve her feelings of anger and hostility toward authority figures. And I realized that I had turned into one of them.

One of the more powerful ways of dealing with people like Mary, especially if the aim is to change their behavior in the long term, is to point out what they are doing when they resort to underhand passive-aggressive patterns. So when Mary resorted to her habitual operational mode, I challenged her. Every time it happened I would say something like, "Mary, it seems to me that you are angry at me. Is that what you are experiencing?" Of course, she would deny any such feelings, often claiming forgetfulness as an excuse (when she hadn't done what she was supposed to do, for example). But as time went on it became increasingly difficult for her to get away with it. Eventually, my very pointed comments seemed to have an effect.

To help Mary understand why she was acting in such a passive-aggressive manner, I also explored with her the nature of her early relationships. Basically, I wanted her to understand the causal relationship between her tendency toward procrastination and the internal resentment she felt toward anyone making a demand on her. While coaching her, it quickly became clear to me that it had been very difficult for Mary to stand up to her authoritarian father. But what might have been a good defensive strategy at 10 years old may no longer be effective at 40. Discussing family dynamics helped Mary understand the reasons why she was the person she was and helped her identify events that triggered certain insecurities, fears, and anxieties. These insights led to a general discussion of the way she dealt with authority figures—including me—and her frequent anger toward me. Although she initially denied there was anger, she eventually became more prepared to acknowledge it.

During our coaching sessions, I was always very careful not to square up directly to Mary's defenses. With people like Mary, you should never argue or correct their denials, but back quietly away, leaving them to reflect on your comments. My motto has always been "Strike when the iron is cold": I will wait to make a point when I see the right opening. I have learned from experience that the first rule for dealing with passive-aggressives is to refrain from getting into a power struggle. They have had a lifetime's practice and it's not a struggle you can win.

For passive-aggressives, arguing is an invitation to see themselves as victims, which makes you the bad guy. By simply sharing my awareness of Mary's covert anger, I was giving her the message that her passive-aggressive style was not the way to deal effectively with interpersonal relationships. Every time I recognized Mary's covert irritation, I would describe calmly and rationally how I experienced her behavior, pointing out inconsistencies. Trying to see an argument from her point of view also helped me to keep my cool. Empathy—difficult as it may be at times—is essential to the coaching relationship.

When dealing with people like Mary it is helpful to ask them how they would solve or improve the particular situation in which they find themselves. I needed to help Mary become more expressive about her own needs. She needed to learn to be assertive in a direct way and to stop acting underhandedly.

In the beginning, she would hem and haw—as she was accustomed to doing to avoid responsibility. I kept the coaching process up to speed by assigning specific tasks with deadlines, which were put in writing. With passive-aggressives, it is critical to focus on accountability. If Mary didn't deliver, I expressed my disappointment directly, factually, and unemotionally. You have to deal with passive-aggressive behavior upfront; if you don't, you only reinforce it. When I gave Mary feedback I would tell her that her behavior confused me. Why did she continue doing what she was doing? Why not find a better way? If she valued our coaching sessions and wanted them to continue, such behavior had to stop. Every time Mary did something like "forgetting," I would tell her I was disappointed.

I realized that much of Mary's behavior was due to her poor self-image. Very low self-confidence is a general feature of passive-aggressives and is one of the reasons why they shirk responsibility. At root is usually the specific dysfunctional dynamics of the family. I devoted a considerable part of each coaching session to helping Mary acknowledge her strengths: the things she was really good at. I needed to help her build up her self-esteem for the good things she was doing both at home and at the office.

Some of our discussions centered on the way Mary dealt with her husband and children. Discussing the effects of her passive-aggressive style on them was another weapon in my armory. I explored how her style affected her children and what the consequences would be. After all, she wanted them to be happy, but the way she was treating them was not exactly a prescription for happiness.

The coaching intervention with Mary was not a quick fix. It went on for quite some time. I found working with her quite a challenge, although amusing at times. Luckily, some of her behavior patterns also started to strike her as comical. As time passed, Mary took the first baby steps of trying to interact with people in a different way. She would practice expressing her irritation in a more direct manner, and then report her successes and failures back to me. And as she generally liked the results, she gained the assurance to continue on the path she had taken. Eventually, I told her I was confident she could go on without my help and saw her only a few times afterwards, as a sort of check-up that she had not reverted to her old dysfunctional patterns.

9

The Obsessive-Compulsive Executive

I am doomed to an eternity of compulsive work. No set goal achieved satisfies. Success only breeds a new goal. The golden apple devoured has seeds. It is endless.

—*Bette Davis*

When you're obsessive, like me, searching for something unattainable can become unhealthy … It's like falling through the air and grabbing at the clouds.

—*Jonny Wilkinson*

I have got this obsessive compulsive disorder where I have to have everything in a straight line, or everything has to be in pairs.

—*David Beckham*

You will encounter many executives displaying obsessive-compulsive behavior in your coaching work—organizations are packed with them. They are the ones known for their orderliness, control, and perfectionism. Their own strict standards color the way they look at the world, which for them is the only "right" one, and their adherence to rules, systems, and orderly structures is inflexible. Obsessive-compulsives seem to be preoccupied with work at the expense of playfulness, adaptability, openness, and efficiency. Predictably, this behavior doesn't make for relaxed or close interpersonal relationships. They can be very stubborn and are unreceptive to other ways of doing things.

As you might expect, trust is a big issue for obsessive-compulsives and explains their difficulty in delegating and sharing responsibilities. Interestingly, while they are resistant to the authority of others, they simultaneously demand that others conform to their way of doing things. Their perfectionism becomes especially troublesome when it begins to interfere with their ability to complete tasks. They are obsessed with getting things right, to the point where they cannot tolerate the possibility of having made a mistake. So, when rules and established procedures do not determine a "correct" answer, decision-making may turn into a time-consuming, long-drawn-out, and often painful process. Obsessive-compulsives may have such difficulty in deciding which tasks should take priority, or the best way of doing a particular task, that they never get started on anything. Unsurprisingly, this mindset leads to procrastination and indecisiveness.

If you have some familiarity with obsessive-compulsives, you will have noticed that they express affection in a highly controlled or stilted manner and are uncomfortable in the presence of people who are emotionally expressive. Stylistically, they come across as emotionally cold and detached, especially in situations they can't control. As you might imagine, obsessive-compulsives don't have great social skills. They lack the kind of playfulness that would enable them to be more in tune with others, and are quite incapable of interpreting the subtle cues that occur within their social environment. Their *Besserwisser* (smart aleck) attitude hardly helps. It interferes with their ability to form close relationships—after all, who likes a know-all?

So what are the origins of this kind of behavior pattern? Most developmental psychologists subscribe to some kind of biopsychosocial model of causation, meaning that this behavior is likely due to biological/genetic, social, and psychological factors. These encompass the way children interact with family members and other children during their early development, and the way the growing child's environment and acquired skills shape its personality and temperament. Faulty parenting has often been viewed as a major factor in the development of this quirky personality type. Healthy emotional development very much depends on two important variables: parental warmth and "good-enough" responsiveness to a child's needs. When these are present, a child feels secure and appropriately valued. When they are absent, problems may follow. For example, clients with obsessive-compulsive characteristics have told me about parents who were emotionally withholding and either over-protective or over-controlling. Some were punished by their parents for every transgression, however slight, while rewards never formed part of this particular socialization package. This type of parenting is obviously not a prescription for *joie de vivre*, spontaneity, or independent thought. Obsessive-compulsive behavior—a child's preferred strategy for avoiding punishment—is a highly likely outcome of having been exposed to such treatment. What's more, children subjected to this type of upbringing are very likely to swallow the anger they feel toward their parents while treating others under their control—like younger siblings—quite harshly. This is a form of identifying with their aggressor, copying the behavior of the people who trouble them. I have also observed that people with this kind of personality problem are prone to pass it on their children.

I was asked to coach an executive who was a very representative example of the kind of person you might encounter with this behavior pattern. The chairman of a biochemical company I had worked with in the past asked me if I would talk to the new CEO, who had recently been hired, to help him get up and running in his new position. The chairman was worried that things were not moving as quickly as had been expected. He explained that William (the new CEO) came from a very different industry. Perhaps, as I was familiar with the organization, I could help him with a somewhat belated onboarding process. Assuming William agreed to be coached, he had to acquire the knowledge, skills, and behaviors needed to become more effective in the new job—and fast.

I asked the chairman to elaborate why he thought my input would be helpful. He replied that, having worked with William for 30 days, he was wondering whether the board had made the right choice of CEO, even though William had stood out from the other candidates during the interview process. The way he was leading the corporation made the chairman wonder whether he would turn out to be a good fit after all. He wasn't convinced that William could adapt to the corporate culture. Of course, he came from a different background, but it was more than that: William came across as inflexible, very set in his ways, and a bad listener. He was obviously a high achiever, hard driving, competitive, and very action oriented, but when it came to decisions, it was very much "my way or the highway." Since his arrival, there had been too much analysis paralysis. When others refused to yield to William's "correct perspective," it led to tension and discord. William also became upset when other people interfered with his rigid routines. The chairman added that some of the key players in the company, whom he'd known for a long time, had complained to him about William's behavior.

From previous experience, I knew that many new CEOs fall at the first hurdle due to unclear or unrealistic expectations, their failure to build partnerships with key stakeholders, their inability to understand the corporate culture of the company or industry, their inability to gain commitment from direct reports, and their failure to recognize and manage the impact of change on the people working for them. I doubted whether I could really help to better William's initial experience in the company. Nevertheless, I told the chairman that if William wanted to talk to me I would make myself available. It's never a good idea to force someone to see a coach.

William called the very next day and asked if we could have lunch together. He said that the chairman had told him that it would be a good idea for us to meet. We set a date to see each other at his office, where the lunch would be held.

At our first meeting William was far from relaxed. He was quite formal, and responded rather stiffly to the few pleasantries I made. I was used to people reacting more playfully. Looking around the office, I registered how meticulously everything was arranged. Nothing seemed to be out of place. I felt that the only concession William made to create a more relaxed impression was to loosen his tie. It was clearly important to him to have things under control. Logic and intellect ruled his conversation.

Listening to him—and later on seeing him in action in meetings—I was struck by his preoccupation with orderliness, perfectionism, and mental and interpersonal control, at the expense of flexibility, openness, and efficiency. He also seemed to have no sense of fun.

In spite of his martinet-like qualities, I rather warmed to William. I viewed his willingness to confide in me about his anxiety over his new job as a good sign for our potential working alliance. He realized that all was not well. Deep down, he knew that his chairman was right, and that he needed some help. What he didn't know was how to go about it, how to change his way of doing things. He was too much stuck in his ways. Interestingly, he seemed to be afraid that unless things were arranged perfectly, disaster would strike. It became clear during our conversations that William was inclined to resort to catastrophizing: a habit of automatically assuming a worst-case scenario and inappropriately characterizing minor or moderate problems or issues as catastrophic events.

I was surprised, however, to realize that William seemed unaware of the discomfort that his stubbornness and rigidity caused other people. He seemed to grasp that if he didn't make a number of changes to his leadership style, his tenure could turn out to be very short—but this understanding was only subliminal. When I prompted him, he acknowledged that he had difficulty adjusting to the much more free-flowing way of doing things in his present environment. He said he found it hard to accept that his role was so very different from the one he had had in his previous organization. He also mentioned that he had a hard time controlling his anger in situations where he felt things were out of control. He was also confused about his status relative to the chairman. The division of labor between chairman and CEO in the company was rather vague and he found this lack of clarity troubling. It seemed to disrupt his orderly mind. When I asked for an example, he recounted an incident when the chairman had directly approached one of his subordinates about a minor issue. That had irritated him deeply; he thought that kind of bypassing was unacceptable.

I should say at this point that I have had considerable experience in coaching people with these characteristics. Obsessive-compulsives are especially attentive to their relative status in dominance-submission relationships. But compared to some of the other types I have described here, they aren't the most difficult people to coach and the prospect is usually much better for them than for other conflict-prone individuals. Having said that, don't be fooled into thinking that working with obsessive-compulsives is a walk in the park. Their need to control—including controlling the coaching process—can sometimes be hard to take. Generally, however, I have found that insight-oriented psychodynamic coaching combined with various cognitive-behavioral interventions can be very productive. You should be aware of the presence of secondary symptoms, such as anxiety and depression, which frequently accompany this condition and can often be treated with antidepressants.

After our lunch, William and I set up a coaching arrangement whereby I would see him every two weeks with the possibility of phone conversations between sessions. It would be a contract for six months, with the option of renewal after that period if we both felt that would be desirable. And so we started.

I have to admit that I enjoyed working with William, but at times his circular argumentation got to me. He seemed to go on forever, repeating the same logic but with no resolution. In these instances, I found it hard work not to be emotionally run down. When I reached my wits' end, I would point out to him that in the general scheme of things I was an outsider. "How," I asked him, "do the people who work for you deal with your logic when you go into this mental overdrive? Can you imagine how devastating your behavior could be to relationships?" I got the impression that my comment made him think. It did at least stop his flow of words.

I also pointed out to William that living up to his perfectionist standards wasn't easy. I found it difficult, anyway. I reminded him of something he'd told me—that, in the past, he would break off relationships when things didn't go the way he wanted. Was he going to do the same thing with me, I asked? And while we were talking about it, could he accept that nobody is perfect? I also added that I wondered if, in the future, it wouldn't be better to learn how to manage whatever caused conflict, rather than responding by terminating a relationship? I have learned from experience that playing out conflict resolution in the course of the coaching process can be a very powerful intervention.

As William's obsession with control was his Achilles heel, I also decided to give him "homework," experimenting with different ways of dealing with the people he worked with. I needed to make him understand that his preoccupation with details, rules, lists, order, organization, and schedules was so all-encompassing that the major point of the activities that needed to be addressed was getting lost. A case in point was his agenda, where I discovered, studying it, that no minute in the day was unaccounted for. I suggested to William that he needed to create free time for himself— time to think. I explored with him how his perfectionism was interfering with the completion of every task he undertook. I felt it was important for him to learn the meaning of "good enough." Everything did not always need to be perfect. At the same time, the challenge remained of how to reduce his level of anxiety, which was increased by my asking him to try to behave differently.

A good example of William's need for perfection was the strategy document required for the annual board meeting. I told him that I wondered how many times he thought this document had to be rewritten. The way he was tinkering with it, asking for rewrite after rewrite, was an ideal way to drive his subordinates crazy. In the meantime, the board meeting was approaching and the members of the board were not going to receive the information they needed in time. I also pointed out to him that although he may have been very talented at strategic planning in the past, he was now CEO, and should let others get on with it, and not hang over their shoulders telling them exactly what needed to be done. He should be much bolder in his efforts at delegation. Of course, I added, it was very likely that people would make mistakes, but wasn't that the only way they would learn? He should be much more of a coach to his people than a controller.

Then I took a different tack, pointing out to William that his workaholism came at the cost of leisure activities and friendships. Where were his friends? Did he even have any? And if he did, had he any time for them? I told him that from what I could see his life was all work and no play. His time management meant there was no time allowed for relaxation. How long could that go on before he had a nervous breakdown? He should try to make an effort to maintain a proper balance between work and other activities.

In particular, I felt William needed to spend more time with his family. From what he told me, what masqueraded as family life sounded more like some kind of business arrangement. He seemed to have no real intimacy with his wife. The only time they did things together was when she attended a company function. His over-controlling style appeared to be a problem not only at work but also at home.

I questioned William further about this and he admitted that things were not good at home. He mumbled something about his difficulty in expressing affection, which brought up the topic of how he dealt with conflict. When he and his wife quarreled, he habitually withdrew, as a defensive measure, apparently to reduce the risk of rejection, accountability, criticism, or exposure. As we explored his family life, I came to realize that I had an ally in his wife, who had recently given him an ultimatum to "get help or get out." It was not just the chairman who felt that he needed help.

Apart from William's difficulty in handling intimacy, his general perfectionist approach didn't help the relationship. His wife complained that she was expected to run the house like a tight ship—in particular by keeping the children in line (seen but not heard). He added that his wife had told him that she felt burdened by his daily scrutiny, his harsh feedback when something he didn't like happened at home, and his low mood. She maintained that his way of relating had a very negative effect on the family dynamics. This last comment was particularly timely, as William had confided in me about his very strained relationship with his oldest son. From what he said, I deduced that this son, probably irritated by all the rules and regulations imposed by his father, had gone into rebellious overdrive, having become (paradoxically) uncontrollable. I remembered another occasion when I had complimented him on his daughter's excellent results at school, only to get William's surprising response that there was nothing to celebrate as they were the results she was expected to have. This gave me the opportunity to ask him how he thought his daughter would feel if she'd heard that comment. How did he think she would react? This question helped him think about his way of relating to the members of his family. To add weight to my comment, I also said that, because of his way of interacting with his family, some of his children could acquire behavior patterns similar to his, which (as he knew better than anyone) was not exactly a prescription for happiness. How would he like that to happen?

I extended William's "homework" to include experimenting with new things, tolerating normal disorder, and taking reasonable risks. I wanted him to learn how to manage new situations that demanded flexibility and compromise. I wanted him to be better at delegation and less of a micromanager. He also needed to be more forgiving about his own and other people's performance.

Fortunately, step-by-step, William learned to control himself when events strayed from the way he thought things "should be." He became better at managing his anxiety. Most importantly, however, he became nicer toward himself. He realized that the high standards he set for himself were far beyond the capacity for any human being to fulfill consistently.

As you have probably gathered, what was originally supposed to be a simple onboarding exercise became a much more prolonged, intensive intervention. As it turned out, I saw William for a period of two years. During that time, he came to understand better the emotional issues underlying his controlling behavior. Acquiring these insights helped him to do things differently. I encouraged him to experiment with various forms of relaxation, including taking vacations. Looking back, I admit that it wasn't always easy to help him to learn how to be nicer to himself. But as he did so, he also became nicer to the people around him, including me. He became less obsessed with their performance. As he became less anxious, he also became less of a slave driver, and he became increasingly better at delegation.

As a considerable amount of damage had been done to the dynamics in the family, rebuilding William's relationships at home turned out to be a major effort. I realized that things would never be perfect, given William's lingering tendency to fall back on control and emotional detachment in stressful situations. Increasingly, however, he took a more reflective stand when he found himself in conflictual situations with members of the family. He also benefited from a yoga program in which he and his wife became involved. It became a regular exercise and helped him become more relaxed.

With his change in attitude, William's relationship with the chairman changed for the better and, over time, the two became quite close. His relationships with the key players in the company also changed. They accepted some of his quirks, but were able to push back when necessary. And William gained credibility in the outside world, helped by the company's high levels of profitability.

chapter 10

Love, Play, and Work

Not until we are lost do we begin to understand ourselves.
—Henry David Thoreau

All life is an experiment. The more experiments you make the better.
—Ralph Waldo Emerson

Self-esteem is as important to our well-being as legs are to a table. It is essential for physical and mental health and for happiness.
—Louise Hart

Having read these woes of dysfunctional executives, you will have realized, if you didn't know it already, that life in organizations can be quite stressful. And you may wonder, at times, whether it really has to be that way. Does work have to be stressful? Aren't there more pleasant ways to go about it? What are the things that we, as coaches, can do to create better places to work? Work is, of course, one of the anchors of psychological wellbeing. I'm sure you must have heard of Sigmund Freud's dictum that mental health consists of *lieben und arbeiten*—love and work. Thus in the coaching work we do, we should never forget the degree to which organizations are invested with psychological meaning. We should always keep in mind that accomplishing something tangible through work can give our clients considerable stability in a highly unstable world. Organizations are ideal outlets to help our clients cope with the stresses and strains of daily life.

Given the importance of healthy organizations for individual psychological wellbeing, a major item that should be on the agenda of every executive coach is to help create healthy workplaces that contribute to, and reinforce, our clients' adaptive functioning. Unfortunately, as you may have already discovered, some organizations can make their people sick and cause them great harm. Of course, this process can go both ways, in that there are also some people who can make their organizations sick—I have shared some examples with you here. It is up to us, as coaches, to figure out what is really going on: what is cause and what is effect. It worries me that on occasions toxic organizations turn to coaches to help healthy executives "adapt," if that's the correct word, to their dysfunctional way of doing things. This is a dangerous trap that we should always try to avoid. Socializing healthy executives to make them more suitable for toxic organizations is not only something we should be alert to; it is also highly unethical. But some coaches do fall into this trap, out of either ignorance or greed. Personally, unless I can see a possibility of nursing the place back to health I don't get involved in these kinds of organizations. In our role as executive coaches, what we really should be doing is contributing to the creation of authentizotic organizations: places of work where people feel truly alive, and work at their best.

I devised the term *authentizotic* myself. I constructed it from two Greek words: *authenteekos* and *zoteekos*. The first conveys the idea that the people and the organization are authentic. As a workplace label, authenticity implies that the organization has a compelling connective quality to its people in its vision, mission, culture, and structure. Also, the organization's leadership has communicated clearly and convincingly not only the *how* but also the *why* of what's happening in the organization, revealing meaning in each person's task. In authentic organizations people have a sense of flow; they feel complete and alive.

Zoteekos means "vital to life." In an organizational context I use this term to describe the way people are invigorated by their work. In this kind of organization, the human need for exploration—closely associated with cognition and learning—is met. The *zoteekos* element of authentizotic organizations allows for self-assertion in the workplace and produces a sense of effectiveness, competence, autonomy, initiative, creativity, entrepreneurship, and industry.

I'm convinced that working in authentizotic organizations can be an antidote to stress, increase people's imagination, and, most importantly, contribute to a healthier and more fulfilling existence.

So, creating healthy organizations is one thing, but what about the people in them? What makes for a healthy executive? The answer depends very much on who you ask. When I ask psychiatrists, psychotherapists, psychoanalysts, and, in particular, executive coaches for their reaction to this question, they all say that their role is to help people operate at full capacity. They want to encourage them to gain insights into their goals and motivations, help them better understand their strengths and weaknesses, and prevent them from engaging in self-destructive activities. Their emphasis is on enabling their clients to choose more freely, instead of being completely led by forces that are outside of their awareness.

This answer has a lot of merit, but needs elaboration. From my experience, having coached large numbers of executives, the healthier ones have a certain set of characteristics. Bear in mind, as I list them, that "health" and "illness" should be viewed as points on a spectrum.

Healthy people:

- have a stable sense of identity
- have a great capacity for reality testing
- have mature defense mechanisms (i.e. not primitive modes of denial, splitting, projection, and scapegoating)
- take responsibility for their actions
- are very resourceful
- believe in their own ability to control the events that affect their lives
- have a healthy perception of their body image and functioning
- can handle ambivalence

- experience the full range of emotions
- live intensively
- are passionate about what they do
- can manage anxiety
- usually have a fulfilling sex life
- establish and cultivate relationships
- know how to use help and advice
- have a sense of belonging to a larger community
- deal effectively with issues of dependency, separation, and loss
- have a positive outlook toward the world
- have the capacity for self-observation and self-analysis
- have a predisposition toward self-reflection
- have a sense of playfulness.

Playfulness

Helping your clients play is an essential coaching skill. Play is not just a frivolous activity; it is engraved in us as part of our genetic make-up. Play has always been an intricate part of the evolution of *Homo sapiens* and through it we have developed as a species. In play, connections between the individual and the environment unfold or emerge, helping us to develop effective learning strategies. Play accentuates our biological tendency to symbolize and create meaning in order to understand the world around us. It is the foundation of language, myths, rituals, behavior, and meaning. Play, artistic expression, creativity, and evolutionary human development are closely allied. For our ancestors, the capacity to play was an essential element of survival and I would go so far as to say that that's still true today. If our life is all work and no play, we really are in trouble. The lack of play is an invitation to stress disorders and mental health problems. Thus, to repeat myself once more, as a coach, you should always find ways to encourage the play element present in your clients.

If you are a parent, you will have seen at first hand that children learn and develop mentally, physically, and socially through play. Play stimulates their imagination and rouses their curiosity, leading to discovery, creativity, and innovation. In play, affective, cognitive, and motivational processes are set into motion. Play ignites creativity and spontaneity and facilitates expressive language and divergent thinking. It helps bridge the gap between concrete experience and abstract thought. Play also gives the opportunity to act out negative emotions and control impulsive behavior. It offers children—and also adults—the chance to experiment with new roles and to explore the intricacies of interpersonal relationships. It helps us understand the meaning of empathy. The give-and-take of play is a context for learning cooperation, initiative, and social and leadership skills. Through play, we learn how to work together, to follow mutually agreed rules, and how to socialize in groups. Play can work wonders for interpersonal relationships. Compassion, trust, and the capacity for intimacy come to the fore through regular play. You must have discovered for yourself that it's difficult to stay mad at someone with whom you play. Through play we learn how to transform emotionally difficult situations into manageable ones. What's more, play helps relieve stress. When we play vigorously, we trigger a mix of endorphins that lift our spirits and help us cope with pain, fear, and anxiety. Play can also have a restorative function in managing grief. But above all, we play for pure pleasure. In fact the benefits of play are too numerous to mention, which makes play not only a seemingly frivolous, but also a very serious, business.

I have dwelled on the importance of play as a prelude to introducing the idea of using play in coaching. Play shouldn't be seen as a lost cause in adulthood. You may not always recognize it, but it is present in many forms, from storytelling, mimicry, and games, to extreme sports like skydiving, high-speed racing, mountain hunting, and so on. Some professions—architecture, design, and acting, for example—are really creative play at work. If, as coaches, we manage to encourage our clients to play with the joyful abandon of childhood, they will continue to reap the benefits throughout their lives. Experience tells us over and over again that there is a strong relationship between playfulness and creativity.

I doubt whether, as coaches, we sufficiently recognize the importance of play to help our clients grow and develop. If we ourselves were more playful and could help our clients rediscover play, would they be much more creatively effective? I think so, and I always try to do so myself. I go to great lengths to make my clients more playful, on the basis of the four Ms, which stand for Me-time, Make-believe, Mastery, and Meaning.

M1 Me-time

Me-time is one of the basic ingredients of play, which is, first and foremost, a representation of freedom. Think about how it feels when you have a great deal of freedom to decide how and when you do your work. Doesn't work become more like play then, even (in fact, especially) when it is highly complex? By me-time I mean having greater autonomy and a free choice. Formally, me-time can be defined as having an internally perceived locus of causality—that is, being able to do what you want to do, rather than what others expect you to do. In situations where you have to do what others tell you, you rarely experience such work as play. But when work is done for its own sake, it gives you a special feeling of liberty. Playing means being self-governed—being able to make your own informed decisions and choosing to act according to your own values and beliefs. Play draws and fascinates us precisely because it's structured by rules that we ourselves (not others) invent or accept. The ultimate freedom in play (and a crucial aspect of its definition) is the freedom to quit. Without that freedom, the rules of play would be intolerable.

M2 Make-believe

An apparent paradox of play is that it's serious yet not serious, real yet not real. Play is centered on make-believe, the pretense that what is not real, is. Make-believe lies at the intersection of cognitive development and social experience. In this way it creates a double consciousness that consists of reality and the representation of reality needed for play. For example, we cannot ride an elephant unless there is a real elephant available for us to ride. But when we are playing, if the rules of the game designate the arm of the sofa as an elephant, we can ride an elephant to our heart's content. In reality, a rug is a piece of material covering the floor, but in play it can be a flying carpet. The fictional situation dictates the rules of the game;

the actual physical world within which the game is played becomes secondary. Because play takes place in a fantasy world, it is governed by the rules in the minds of the players rather than externally imposed rules. But what's fascinating is that this make-believe world offers great developmental opportunities. For example, within it, children can override their fears; they can fight off dragons with magical swords; they can vanquish the monsters under the bed; they can be masters of the universe. Through play children acquire control of the world, as opposed to being subject to its vagaries. I believe the same effect can be achieved by play in adulthood. Make-believe play can have a huge cognitive and emotional impact, allowing your clients to experiment with social roles and interactions. Play (sometimes described as "homework") helps your clients practice walking in others' shoes. The urge to make believe accompanies us throughout life. Just as in childhood, your clients' daydreams help them define future plans and aspirations by allowing them to play with various roles, lifestyles, and occupations. And these daydreams are fundamental to the creative process.

M3 Mastery

All of us like to experience a sense of competence, the ability to interact effectively with the environment. Again, this desire can be seen very clearly, starting with children's play. Children will gravitate to areas in which they perceive competence and avoid areas where success is hit or miss, or there is no sense of accomplishment. As might be expected, successful and failed attempts at mastery result in reinforcement of the domain toward which a person migrates. Interactive play and games provide opportunities for experimentation and are a way of achieving a sense of mastery over the environment. Again, this motivation to play exists *within* the individual rather than being dependent on any external pressure. The goals are experienced as an intrinsic part of the game, not as the sole reason for engaging in the game's actions. Thus the main objective in such play is *creating* the object, not having it. For example, when my children play on the beach, busily trying to create a sandcastle, I'm sure that they wouldn't be pleased if I said, "I'll make the castle for you." That would spoil their fun completely. It's the process, not the product, that motivates them. It's the mastery of making sandcastles that counts; the significant element is the efficacy of doing it. This pride in mastery continues into adulthood, and is something we should leverage while coaching our clients.

M4 Meaning

Some of the most fundamental questions our clients will ask themselves are "Who am I?," "Where do I come from?," and "What is the purpose of my life?" This is a personalization of the more general question, "What is the meaning of life, the universe, and everything?" Behind all these questions, of course, looms the specter of death.

All meaning in life is self-defined, and, as might be expected, the meaning of life is different for different people. Things and situations in our lives have no meaning by themselves; we attribute meaning to them, depending on our perspective, reality, and belief system. Something that has deep meaning for you might be meaningless to other people, or have different meanings to them at different times in their lives, depending on their experiences, motivations, beliefs, and perspectives.

Meaning implies experiencing the world by interacting authentically with our environment and with others—giving something to the world through self-expression. Our clients may become depressed, however, when there is a mismatch between their lived and desired experience; between the meaninglessness of everyday life and their innate drive to search for meaning, to self-actualize, to be all that they can be. Here, once again, play takes on an essential role in the search for meaning. It's critical to their exploration of facets of their identity and the various roles they might undertake or consider undertaking. In that respect, meaning is both created and found. It also needs to be an essential part of the coaching process.

The Group Coaching Intervention

As executive coaches, we need to help our clients practice self-control, but also help them play. How can we help them to become sufficiently self-aware to remain playful, without that self-awareness (and the accompanying sense of responsibility) inhibiting that very playfulness? What can we do to make play once more a central part of their lives? As coaches, how can we create the kind of space that enables them to do so?

I consider that one of my roles as an executive coach is to bring my clients to a place where they can play more fully; where they can engage in a dialectic, interactive process that enables them to experiment, and also to have both the freedom and the discipline to cultivate a sense of possibility and enhanced meaning. One way of doing this effectively is through various forms of group coaching.

However, getting there isn't that easy. We may think that our clients need help, but they don't necessarily realize it themselves. How prepared are they to "play"? It's most helpful, of course, when people volunteer. Most of my clients want to participate because they sense that something is going on in their lives that they need time out to explore. They are mentally ready to do things differently. They have not only come to the realization that they are at a dead end, but they also want to do something about it.

But even when this is the case, I find that executives need to summon up a considerable amount of courage in order to join in. While I try to help them rediscover their childlike willingness to try something new, they are often held back by their fear of making a fool of themselves. There is a lot of posturing in adulthood. Many adults consciously suppress their playful self, on the grounds that life is too serious for play. This may be existentially true, but we don't get anywhere if we are caught up in such negative thoughts. Such a state of mind destroys the capacity for playfulness.

But I have found that the technology of educational play can be extremely helpful to further the creative development of my clients. I have discovered that group coaching with a psychodynamic orientation sets the stage for the kinds of playful intervention that foster learning, enhance relationships, and improve health and wellbeing. This form of play provides a safe space in which adults can take the opportunity to experiment, embark on new life experiences, rediscover their creativity, and even reinvent and renew themselves. Let me give you an example of the kind of CEO "recycling" that group coaching can offer.

INSEAD, the international business school that is headquartered near Paris in France, with further campuses in Singapore and Abu Dhabi, probably does more group coaching than any other institution in the world—most of them short interventions. Once a year, I run a workshop at INSEAD called "The Challenge of Leadership: Creating Reflective Leaders." Twenty very senior executives (most of them CEOs from the private and public sectors and from all over the world) are invited to participate. These executives apply to the program for a variety of reasons. The guiding themes may have to do with seemingly insoluble dilemmas, negative feelings about themselves, being bored, or feeling like an impostor. They may also be suffering from a variety of stress symptoms, or struggling with the existential dilemmas of life. Typically, however, these issues are not always clearly articulated in the candidates' minds when they apply to the program.

To be accepted to the program, each potential participant has to complete a complex application form with many personal questions. The information provided helps me to make an initial assessment of the candidate's suitability for the program. In addition, I interview each future participant— wherever their location—in person (or over the phone) to see if they have what it takes to go through such a challenging coaching activity, where the "life" case study will be a main source of interpretive material. In these interviews, I look for signs of psychological mindedness, the candidates' capacity to be open and responsive, their degree of defensiveness, their sense of who they are, their capacity for reality testing, and their preparedness to really understand themselves better.

The workshop consists of three 5-day modules with breaks of approximately two months in between. Six months after the last of these modules, a fourth 4-day module assesses how well the participants have enacted the life decisions they made over the duration of the first three modules. The expectation is that during each module the participants learn more about themselves, agree a "contract" on what to work on in the workplace and at home during the time they are away from the workshop, and return to the workshop to deepen their understanding. Mutual coaching is part of the program design and fellow participants monitor "homework" assignments. Participants write reflection papers after each module describing how they have experienced the process. These are sent to me, and provide essential feedback on the participants' experience. But they also serve an additional function, in that writing about our experiences is a life-structuring exercise in itself.

The first module is the most structured of the four. During this module I give a number of interactive mini-lectures on high-performance organizations, organizational culture, leadership (exemplary and dysfunctional), the career life cycle, cross-cultural management, organizational stress, constructive feedback practices, and the dynamics of individual and organizational change. However, the central model of psychological activity and organization within the program is the personal case history. At some point, each participant is expected to volunteer to sit in the "hot seat" to discuss his or her salient life issues and dilemmas. This part of the program is extremely important, as experiences and decisions, including successes and setbacks, become organized when people narrate their personal life story. The presentation becomes a process of self-discovery, and also helps the other participants to understand better the problems they have in their own public or private life.

During the second module a considerable amount of time is devoted to processing a number of 360-degree feedback instruments that I have developed. All of these have both an organizational, team, and personal focus, including feedback gathered from spouses/partners, or significant other(s). Additional information is collected from other family members and close friends. (I call this process not 360-degree feedback but 720-degree.) This information provides the basis for a more refined action plan in the period between the second and third modules. The main focus of the third week is the consolidation of acquired insights, the creation of tipping points for change, and experimentation with future action plans.

Throughout the program, a key element is nurturing a sense of play among the participants. To enable this playfulness to come to the fore, an essential task for the coach is to create a safe, transitional space that is characterized by trust and reciprocity. This space will provide a kind of holding environment in which the participants (depending on the dysfunctionalities they have to overcome) can be contained and mirrored. A holding environment of this kind is necessary to be able to begin experimentation, play, and working through their issues.

By the third week of this program, most of the participants know each other better than many of their family members do. At this point the interchange in the plenary session has become extremely free-flowing, with much less intervention required from me. The group of participants begins to turn into a self-analyzing community. Finally, the fourth week of the program is a sort of built-in alumni session, providing an opportunity to see if all the learning has been internalized.

The key factor in this kind of group coaching program is creating opportunities for the participants to "play." For example, a very effective way to start this "play" is to ask each of them to draw a self-portrait. This enables them to reflect on how they would portray their life in images. This exercise has proven to be extremely helpful in having the participants enter a different world of make-believe. After some initial hesitation, they all become enthusiastic about it. To create the safe, transitional space that these interventions require, the coach has to demonstrate authenticity, directed empathy, and unconditional positive regard while being engaged with the participants. Once such a space has been created, it will support a learning community in which the participants will dare to experiment with new possibilities and life strategies.

I can't emphasize strongly enough that the creation of this transitional space is vital for the development of the participants, helping them to obtain insight into their inhibitions and their capacity to create. This space will also provide some kind of "container" for the participants, allowing them to get rid of their "garbage," by which I mean the various undigested feelings they're trying to metabolize. Only when they feel this containment is adequate—having acquired trust in the process—will they feel secure enough to begin experimentation, and play, and work through their issues. Experimenting with alternatives, and experiencing satisfactory results, enables participants in this kind of program to make connections between inner and outer reality. These links will create a greater sense of authenticity and efficacy.

These experiments in new beginnings are helped by the fact that the participants spend a considerable amount of time in small groups inside and outside the classroom. These playful interactions are extremely valuable, as these encounters serve to consolidate newly acquired behavioral patterns. Learning from the others is essential to making this process of change work. Eventually, the participants in these organizational group coaching sessions form an intense learning community in which each of them gives the others constructive feedback (nobody should get hurt, but no "love bombing" either) whenever they fall back into behavior patterns they are trying to unlearn. The important challenge is to turn the participating groups into self-analyzing communities.

In the later stages of the workshop, the members of this now playful learning community demonstrate a remarkable level of emotional intelligence, compared with their abilities in the first module. In many instances, the program learning becomes even more consolidated through follow-up sessions year after year, which offers the opportunity to assess the degree to which new behavior patterns have become part of their *modus operandi*.

The Psychological Dance

When you help your clients relearn how to play, it's important that they focus their attention on the sensations, feelings and thoughts they had not previously acknowledged. I always ask them how they *feel* when listening to a presentation. I want them to pay attention to feelings, not merely cognitions. As a coach, you need to help your clients become more aware of their feelings and how their feelings influence their behavior and actions. You should also bear in mind that this kind of facilitation goes both ways. To be sufficiently susceptible to what is happening to your clients, you also need to be highly vigilant about your own counter-transference reactions—how *you* experience the comments your clients are making. In addition, when listening to the narratives that emerge, you also need to listen to what's *not* being said. To sum up, the process is a playful dance between your clients, the observations of the group-as-a-whole, and the way you will experience this interplay. The free play of attention stimulates cognitive flow, emotional resilience, and physical alertness. While the dance is played out, you should try to ensure that every one of the clients who speaks up is listened to respectfully and that everyone has the opportunity to be heard. To make the process work, I also encourage everyone to articulate what he or she really thinks, not hold back. They should say what they feel should be said, but in a respectful manner. This means that there will be negative reflections; the elephants in the room will have to be named. The clients are encouraged to express their feelings about the process, which will range between sadness, anger, joy, despondency, disgust, excitement, and envy.

Everyone enters a process like these group coaching interventions in order to be seen and understood, but at the same time they also fear criticism and exposure. Also, some of your clients may not know how to pay the same attention to others, without projecting their positive and negative fantasies onto them. Play, however, helps develop practices that cultivate high-quality attention and awareness, both of themselves and others.

As the coaching process progresses the participants tend to take deep personal responsibility for themselves, and for what the group presents to them. Within the safe space of the workshop, unconscious and unrecognized material, including long-repressed fears and longings, will surface, prompting classic forms of resistance, such as splitting, projection, denial, displacement, dissociation, and depression. As time goes on, these defenses become less effective. The group context creates feelings of intimacy, belonging, and social healing and becomes a container for individuals' cathartic experiences.

Your help may also be needed in helping your clients re-enter their daily lives when the group sessions are over. They need to take their new insights and learning with them, and find a new fit for these in the habitual personal and work environment. This means using their thoughts, feelings, and even their bodies differently, and demonstrating this difference in their daily behavior. Change has to be manifested if it is to be real, but it has to be practiced until it is lodged in each client's behavioral repertoire. If not, it will dissipate, like a mirage.

chapter 11

You Will Meet a Tall, Dark Stranger

If you're not failing every now and again, it's a sign you're not doing anything very innovative.

— *Woody Allen*

Confidence is contagious. So is lack of confidence.

— *Vince Lombardi*

Show me someone who has done something worthwhile, and I'll show you someone who has overcome adversity.

— *Lou Holz*

"You will meet a tall, dark stranger" is the fortune-teller's clichéd prediction. As an executive coach, you will meet many strangers—whether they are tall and dark is another matter. Your real challenge in every case will be to make them less of a stranger to themselves and to you. In this book, I have described some of the "strangers"—in the form of difficult and even toxic individuals—you may encounter in your work.

It's not always easy to do the work we do, but the work is interesting and very important, as these "strangers" act out their private quirks on a public stage. Many executives cannot really manage, as they don't recognize the power of the intrapsychic and interpersonal forces that are derailing them. They may be prone to paranoia and depression, lose touch with reality, and leave a mess wherever they go. Fortunately, most of them have sufficient strength of character and coping abilities to prevent this from happening. They possess the inner resources to manage the pressures that come with senior executive positions.

In spite of obvious dysfunctionality, some companies support (and are even breeding grounds for) toxic leaders. People with certain emotional disturbances—narcissists or bullies, for example—may be held up as models of highly successful executives. While considered pathologically sick, they function well because their symptoms are adaptive, reinforced, or actually required by their job and its demands. In the meantime, such executives make the healthy people around them unwell.

Your role as an executive coach is to do everything in your power to prevent people from being driven crazy. Dysfunctionalities are ever-present. To spot the danger signs, executive coaches take on the role of sparring partner to test how well their clients resist the temptations that bring out their darker side. You may need to take on the role of the wise fool—the kind of fool who tried to save King Lear from himself—giving your clients feedback on things like their accessibility, their need to blow their own horn, the way they react to bad news, how effective they think they are in emotional management, how mature they are in using their defenses, and how good they are at reality testing.

Many of the complex and even toxic executives you encounter will prove difficult or even unable to change. Many of them feel no need to change; they are not in enough "pain." But, as the saying goes, "No pain, no gain": if there is pain, are they willing to take a hard look at themselves? Are they prepared to delve into the deeper meaning of their actions?

Even if they seem amenable to the coaching process, trying to change them will often be an uphill battle. Many prefer to remain blind and deaf to whatever is happening around them. It will not be easy for you to help them understand the extent to which they, and ultimately their organizations, are the cause of whatever problems they are experiencing. The upside is that if they understand the need to change, executive coaching can go a long way to help them change whatever they are doing.

Sigmund Freud once told the novelist Stefan Zweig that all his life he had been "struggling with the demon"—the demon of irrationality. Wise executives realize that this demon causes problems. It's your role as an executive coach to point out the extent to which unconscious, seemingly irrational processes, can affect your clients' behavior. You should help them recognize the limits of irrationality and make an effort to understand their character traits. Executives who fail to recognize their irrational side are like ships faced with an iceberg, forgetting that the greatest danger lies below the surface. Effective executives, however, are those who know how to combine reflection with action by using self-insight as a restraining force when the sirens of power are calling. It's here that you, as an executive coach, can play a defining role.

Appendix: A Short Note on Coaching Interventions

For simplicity and clarity, I have omitted references to theory in the main text of this book. However, a short note is needed to tell you something about the most commonly used approaches to coaching. The existing literature might suggest that the varieties of coaching orientations are endless. Don't worry. If you take a more than cursory look, you will discover that most of the presenting schools of thought are variations on a limited number of theoretical conceptualizations. You may find that many of these new, supposedly innovative approaches, add very little (if anything) that's truly new. If you take a second look, you will discover that most only expand on existing approaches, or combine aspects of a number of them. You will find that there is a considerable amount of overlap.

The majority of executive coaches subscribe to two main streams of thought—*psychodynamic* and *cognitive-behavioral*. While the first orientation pays a considerable amount of attention to the client's past history (exploring the reasons for present-day problem behavior), the second disregards the past entirely, to focus on challenges that need to be taken care of in the present and the future.

Confused? I'm not surprised. Both forms of executive coaching can be quite successful, because both approaches try to accomplish the same thing: to help executives who struggle with contemporary issues in their lives to function more effectively. To the best of my understanding, the ultimate aim of both approaches is to help their clients regain a sense of control and pleasure in life. Given this basic premise, the use of one approach or the other very much depends on individual coaches' training, style, and personality. Some coaches use only one approach with all their clients; some tend to be more eclectic; and others tailor their approach based on a particular client's needs, symptoms, and personality. I have learned from personal experience that adhering rigidly to one way of coaching can backfire.

People who prefer the psychodynamic approach try to help executives acquire increased self-knowledge and a deeper understanding of their relationships with others. To accomplish this, they acknowledge that a great deal of our behavior is unconscious and take into consideration that our personal history deeply impacts the way we think, feel, and act in the present. Their main focus will be to find the hidden feelings and motives that we all have to help resolve unconscious conflicts shown in present behavior. To discover these links, psychodynamically oriented coaches explore how events that have happened in early life have affected the way their clients think about themselves, how they relate to others, and how they deal with emotions. Through the examination of these unresolved conflicts (the results of dysfunctional relationships from the past), they help their clients acquire a greater understanding of the influence of the past on present behavior—they help them to become more conscious of their unconscious thoughts, feelings, and motives. Having such understanding will help them realize which aspects of those problems they may be able to solve or improve. In this journey of self-exploration, psychodynamically oriented coaches help their clients learn how to take greater control over their lives and respond to challenging situations with healthy coping skills.

The underlying concept behind the cognitive-behavioral approach to coaching is that our thoughts and feelings play a fundamental role in our behavior. According to the advocates of this school of thought, people need to acquire new coping techniques and problem-solving skills in order to change. They suggest that we can overcome our difficulties by identifying and changing dysfunctional patterns of thinking, behavior, and emotional responses. They point out that some of us may be trapped in self-deprecating beliefs that contribute to a vicious cycle of negative thoughts. We need to learn how to recognize and change maladaptive thought patterns and habitual behaviors. For example, we may have patterns of distorted thinking, e.g. excessive self-criticism or guilt ("I always screw up" or "It must be my fault"); catastrophizing ("The situation is so terrible, I can't stand it"); or attributing negative motives to others ("I know everyone dislikes me"). All these make us vulnerable to feeling bad. Cognitive-behavioral coaches aim to help their clients correct or change negative thoughts into positive ones. They may hand out "homework" assignments requiring clients to document their thoughts, classifying them as different kinds of distortions, such as "all-or-nothing thinking," or "jumping to conclusions." The purpose of this approach is to recognize and change maladaptive thought patterns and behaviors, improve the ways people handle their feelings and worries, break the cycle of dysfunctional habitual behaviors, and learn how to respond in more effective ways. Their ultimate objective is to make clients understand that while they can't control every aspect of the world around them, they can take control of how they interpret and deal with things in their environment. This approach is more focused on the "here and now" than the psychodynamic approach.

Advocates of the cognitive-behavioral school of thought make the point that the psychodynamic approach tends to be abstract, indirect, or even impractical compared to their usually briefer interventions. Cognitive-behavioralists are critical of seemingly endless examinations of the past that (they think) don't necessarily translate into behavioral change. In contrast, advocates of the psychodynamic approach argue that there is far more to mental, emotional, and spiritual health than thinking correctly and achieving predefined behavioral outcomes. They believe that their way of intervention will have more durable results than the cognitive-behavioral approach, which may have short-term successes that do not necessarily last.

I can tell you from my own experience that a dogmatic outlook never helps anybody. It's better to tailor the coaching approach to the needs of the individual, which might involve the use of both forms of intervention or a balance of the two at different points in the process.

Whatever approach you use, that you should always pay attention to the systemic elements of a coaching situation. Clients don't function in isolation. They are part of a spider's web of connections. The systems of interaction with their work environment and their family and friends need to be taken into consideration if you are to do your work effectively.

In Chapter 10, I gave an example of a group-oriented coaching intervention. However, many different kinds of group intervention are possible. Some are short, but others (like my CEO seminar) can go on for a considerable amount of time. Group size and economies of scale will be factors. But the financial cost may be less in the case of group coaching, as a number of people are coached at the same time. Another advantage of group coaching is that the participants have not only the coach but also their fellow participants, who can act as agents of change.

There are a number of forces of change in group coaching situations that increase the likelihood that your clients will be helped to deal better with the vicissitudes of life. For example, I have discovered that group coaching can provide participants with a considerable dose of hope, a consequence of noticing how the other people in the group are making better choices in their lives. In addition, presenting your problems to a sympathetic audience can be a very positive, cathartic experience. Also, being part of a group of people with similar backgrounds and experiences helps participants recognize that what they are going through is universal and that they are not alone in their confusion. Furthermore, the members of the group will be able to help each other by sharing information—they are able to share their strengths, and by being a mutual support group, boost their self-confidence. In addition, taking a more "historical" perspective, the group in some ways resembles the family, giving each participant the opportunity to explore how childhood experiences have contributed to their personality make-up and specific types of behavior. If there is enough trust, the group setting can be an ideal place to experiment with new behaviors without too much risk. It can be a comfortable setting in which to practice behaviors that could turn out to be destructive or unhelpful in real life. But by interacting with other people and receiving feedback from the group and the coach, individuals can gain a greater understanding of themselves and learn what works and what doesn't. It also helps participants realize that they are responsible for their own lives, actions, and choices.

Bibliography

(Rather than including references throughout this book, I have compiled here a list of titles that may be helpful to readers who want to pursue further the topics I have discussed)

Acklin, M. W. (1992). Psychodiagnosis of personality structure. Psychotic personality organization, *Journal of Personality Assessment*, 58, 454–463.

Acklin, M. W. (1993). Psychodiagnosis of personality structure II. Borderline personality organization, *Journal of Personality Assessment*, 61, 329–341.

Acklin, M. W. (1994). Psychodiagnosis of personality structure III. Neurotic personality organization, *Journal of Personality Assessment*, 63 (1), 1–9.

Ainsworth, M., Blehar, M., Waters, E. & Wall, S. (1978). *Patterns of Attachment*. Hillsdale, NJ: Erlbaum.

American Psychiatric Association; American Psychiatric Association (2013). *Diagnostic and Statistical Manual of Mental Disorders* (Fifth ed.). Arlington, VA: American Psychiatric Publishing.

American Psychiatric Association (2000). *Diagnostic and Statistical Manual of Mental Disorders (DSM-IV-TR)*. Washington, DC: APA.

Babiak, B. & Hare, R. D. (2006). *Snakes in Suits: When Psychopaths go to Work*. New York: HarperCollins

Bager-Charleson, S. (2010). *Why Therapists Choose to Become Therapists*. London: Karnac.

Bandura, A. (1997). *Self-Efficacy: The Exercise of Control*. New York: W. H. Freeman.

Basch, M. F. (1988). *Understanding Psychotherapy*. New York: Basic Books.

Basch, M. F. (1995). *Doing Brief Psychotherapy*. New York: Basic Books.

Beck, A. T. & Freedman, A. (1990). *Cognitive Therapy of Personality Disorders*. New York: Guilford.

Beck, A. T., Emery, G. & Greenberg, R. L. (2005). *Anxiety Disorders and Phobias: A Cognitive Perspective*. New York: Basic Books.

Blair, R. J., Mitchell, D. R. & Blair, K. (2005). *The Psychopath: Emotion and the Brain*. New York: Wiley-Blackwell.

Bowlby, J. (1969). *Attachment*. Second Edition (Attachment and Loss Series, Vol. 1). New York: Basic Books.

Bowlby, J. (1988). *A Secure Base: Parent-child Attachment and Healthy Human Development*. New York: Basic Books.

Cassidy, J. & Shaver, P. R. (Eds.) (1999). *Handbook of Attachment: Theory, Research, and Clinical Applications*. New York: The Guilford Press.

Crits-Christoph, P. & J. P. Barber (Eds.) (1991). *Handbook of Short-Term Dynamic Psychotherapy*. New York: Basic Books.

Csikszentmihalyi, M. (1990). *Flow: The Psychology of Optimal Experience*. New York: Harper Perennial.

Csikszentmihalyi, M. (1996). *Creativity: Flow and the Psychology of Discovery and Exploration*. New York: Harper Perennial.

Dryden, W. & Spurling, L. (Eds.) (1989). *On Becoming a Psychotherapist*. London: Routledge.

Elkind, D. (2006). *The Power of Play: How Spontaneous, Imaginative Activities Lead to Happier, Healthier Children*. New York: De Capo Press.

Etchegoyen, H. (2005). *The Fundamentals of Psychoanalytic Technique*. London: Karnac Books.

Feltham, C. (Ed.) (1999). *Understanding the Counselling Relationship*. London: Sage

Fenichel, O. (1945). *The Psychoanalytic Theory of Neurosis*. New York: Norton.

Frankl, V. (2006). *Man's Search for Meaning*. Boston: Beacon Press.

Freud, A. *The Ego and the Mechanisms of Defense*. New York: International Universities Press, 1946.

Grant, A. M. & Stober, D. R. (2006). *Evidence-Based Coaching Handbook*. London: John Wiley & Sons Ltd.

Greenberg, J. R. & Mitchell, S. A. (1983). *Object Relations in Psychoanalytic Theory*. Cambridge, Massachusetts: Harvard University Press.

Goleman, D. (1995). *Emotional Intelligence*. London: Bloomsbury.

Griswold, C. (2007). *Forgiveness: A Philosophical Exploration*. Cambridge: Cambridge University Press.

Hare, R. D. (1999). *Without Conscience: The Disturbing World of the Psychopaths Among Us*. New York: The Guilford Press.

Heatherton, T. & Weinberger, J. L. (Eds.) (1994). *Can Personality Change?* Washington, DC: American Psychological Association.

Herve, H. & Yuille, J. C. (Eds.) (2007). *The Psychopath: Theory, Research and Practice*. Mahwah, NJ: Lawrence Erlbaum Associates.

Hogan, R. T. & Johnson, J. (Eds.) (1997). *Handbook of Personality Psychology*. New York: Morgan Kaufman.

Holmes, J. (2001). *The Search for the Secure Base: Attachment Theory and Psychotherapy*. London: Brunner-Routledge.

Horowitz, M. J. (Ed.). (1991). *Person Schemas and Maladaptive Interpersonal Patterns*. Chicago: University of Chicago Press.

Hudson, F. M. (1999). *The Handbook of Coaching: A Comprehensive Resource Guide for Managers, Executives, Consultants, and Human Resource Professionals*. San Francisco, CA: Jossey-Bass.

Huizinga, J. (1955). *Homo Ludens: A Study of the Play-Element in Culture*. Boston: Beacon Press.

Jamison, K. (1997). *The Unquiet Mind*. New York: Picador.

Kegan, R. & Lahey, L. (2009). *Immunity to Change: How to Overcome It and Unlock the Potential in Yourself and Your Organization*. Boston: Harvard Business School Press.

Kernberg, O. (1975). *Borderline Conditions and Pathological Narcissism*. New York: Jason Aronson.

Kernberg, O. (1980). *Internal World and External Reality*. New York: Jason Aronson.

Kets de Vries, M. F. R. (2001). Creating authentizotic organizations: Well-functioning individuals in vibrant companies, *Human Relations*, 54 (1), 101–111.

Kets de Vries, M. F. R. (2001). *The Leadership Mystique*. London: Financial Times/ Prentice Hall.

Kets de Vries, M. F. R. (2004). *The Global Executive Leadership Inventory: Facilitator's Guide*. San Francisco: Pfeiffer.

Kets de Vries, M. F. R. (2005). *Personality Audit: Facilitator's Guide*, Fontainebleau, INSEAD Global Leadership Centre.

Kets de Vries, M. F. R. (2007). Decoding the team conundrum: The eight roles executives play, *Organizational Dynamics*, 36 (1), 28–44.

Kets de Vries, M. F. R. (2009). *Reflections on Leadership and Career Development*. New York: John Wiley & Sons Inc.

Kets de Vries, M. F. R. (2009). *Reflections on Character and Leadership*. West Sussex, UK: Wiley.

Kets de Vries, M. F. R. (2009). *Sex, Money, Happiness and Death: The Quest for Authenticity*. Hampshire, UK: Palgrave.

Kets de Vries, M. F. R. (2010). *Inner Theatre Inventory: Facilitator's Guide*. Fontainebleau, France: INSEAD.

Kets de Vries, M. F. R. (2010). *The Organizational Culture Audit: Facilitator's Guide*. Fontainebleau, France: INSEAD.

Kets de Vries, M. F. R. (2011). *Reflections on Groups and Organisations*. West Sussex, UK: Wiley.

Kets de Vries, M. F. R. (2011). *The Hedgehog Effect: The Secrets of Building High Performance Teams*. New York: Wiley.

Kets de Vries, M. F. R. (2014). *Mindful Leadership Coaching: Journeys into the Interior.* Hampshire, UK: Palgrave.

Kets de Vries, M. F. R. (2014). *The Global Executive Leadership Mirror: Facilitator's Guide.* Fontainebleau, France: INSEAD.

Kets de Vries, M. F. R. & Miller, D. (1984). *The Neurotic Organization: Diagnosing and Changing Counterproductive Styles of Management,* San Francisco, CA: Jossey-Bass.

Kets de Vries, M. F. R., Florent-Treacy, E. & Korotov, K. (2007). *Coach and Couch: The Psychology of Making Better Leaders,* Hampshire: Palgrave Macmillan.

Kets de Vries, M. F. R., Guillen, L., Korotov, K. & Florent-Treacy, E. (2010). *The Coaching Kaleidoscope: Insights from the Inside,* Hampshire: Palgrave Macmillan.

Kilberg, R. R. (2000). *Executive Coaching.* Washington, DC: American Psychological Association.

Kohut, H. (1971). *The Analysis of the Self.* New York: International Universities Press.

Kohut, H. (1977). *The Restoration of the Self.* New York: International Universities Press.

Korotov, K., Florent-Treacy, E., Kets de Vries, M. F. R. & Bernard, A. (2011). *Tricky Coaching.* Hampshire: Palgrave/Macmillan.

Kottler, J. A. (1993). *On Being a Therapist.* San Francisco: Jossey-Bass.

Leichsenring, F. & Leibing, E. (2003). The effectiveness of psychodynamic therapy and cognitive behavior therapy in the treatment of personality disorders: A meta-analysis, *American Journal of Psychiatry,* 160 (7), 1223–1232.

Luborsky, L. & Crits-Cristoph, P. (1998). *Understanding Transference: The Core Conflictual Relationship Theme Method.* Washington, DC: American Psychological Association.

Mahler, M. S., Pine, F. & Bergman, A. (1975). *The Psychological Birth of the Human Infant.* New York: Basic Books.

Malan, D. H. (1976). *The Frontier of Brief Psychotherapy.* New York: Plenum.

Mann, J. (1973). *Time Limited Psychotherapy.* Cambridge, MA: Harvard University Press.

Maroda, K. J. (2004). *The Power of Countertransference.* Hillsdale, NJ: Analytic Press.

McAdams, D. P. (1993). *Stories We Live By: Personal Myths and the Making of the Self.* New York: William Morrow and Company.

McCullough Vaillant, L. (1997). *Changing Character.* New York: Basic Books.

McDougall, J. (1985). *Theaters of the Mind.* New York: Basic Books.

McLeod, J. (1997). *Narrative and Psychotherapy.* London: Sage.

Meissner, W. W. (1978). *The Paranoid Process.* New York: Jason Aronson.

Mikulincer, M. & Shaver, P. R. (2007). *Attachment in Adulthood: Structure, Dynamics, and Change.* New York: Guilford.

Miller, W. R. & Rollnick, S. (2002). *Motivational Interviewing: Preparing People to Change.* New York: Guilford Press.

Millon, T. (1996). *Disorders of Personality: DSM-IV and Beyond.* New York: Wiley.

Millon, T. (2004). *Personality Disorders in Modern Life*. New York: John Wiley.

Millon, T., Simonsen, E. Birket-Smith, M. & Davis, R. (1998). *Psychopathy: Antisocial, Criminal, and Violent Behavior*. New York: Guilford Press.

Munro, A. (1999). *Delusional Disorder: Paranoia and Related Illnesses*. Cambridge: Cambridge University Press.

Palmer, S. & Whybrow, A. (2007). *Handbook of Coaching Psychology: A Guide for Practitioners*. London: Routledge.

Reich, W. (1949). *Character Analysis*. New York: Farrar, Straus and Giroux.

Reik, T. (1983). *Listening with the Third Ear*. New York: Farrar, Straus and Giroux.

Rogers, C. (1951). *Client-centered Therapy: Its Current Practice, Implications and Theory*. London: Constable.

Schaefer, C. (Ed.) (2003). *Foundations of Play Therapy*. Hoboken, NJ: Wiley & Sons, Inc.

Shapiro, D. (1965). *Neurotic Styles*. New York: Basic Books.

Schein, E. H. (1992). *Organizational Culture and Leadership*. San Francisco, CA: Jossey-Bass.

Seligman, M. E. P. (1975). *Helplessness: On Depression, Development and Death*. San Francisco: W. H. Freeman.

Simon, G. K. (1996). *In Sheep's Clothing: Understanding and Dealing with Manipulative People*. Little Rock: A. J. Christopher & Company.

Spence, D. P. (1982). *Narrative Truth and Historical Truth*. New York: Norton.

Storr, A. (1979). *The Art of Psychotherapy*. New York: Methuen.

Strupp, H. H. & J. L. Binder (1984). *Psychotherapy in a New Key: A Guide to Time-Limited Dynamic Psychotherapy*. New York: Basic Books.

Tomb, D. A. & Christensen, D. D. (1987). *Case studies in Psychiatry*. Baltimore: Williams & Wilkins.

Vaillant, G. E. (1992). *Ego Mechanisms of Defense: A Guide to Clinicians and Researchers*. New York: American Psychiatric Publishing.

Weeks, G. R. & L'Abate, L. (1982). *Paradoxical Psychotherapy: Theory and Practice with Individuals, Couples, and Families*. New York: Brunner/Mazel.

White, R. W. (1959). Motivation reconsidered: The concept of competence, *Psychological Review*, 66 (5), 297–333.

Whitmore, J. (2002). *Coaching for Performance: Growing People, Performance and Purpose*. London: Nicholas Brealey Publishing.

Wilson, T. D. (2004). *Strangers to Ourselves: Discovering the Adaptive Unconscious*. New York: The Belknap Press.

Winnicott, D. W. (1971). *Playing and Reality*. London: Tavistock.

Yalom, I. D. (1985). *The Theory and Practice of Group Psychotherapy*. New York, Basic Books.

Zaleznik, A. (1966). *Human Dilemmas of Leadership*. New York: HarperCollins.

Zaleznik, A. & Kets de Vries, M. F. R. (1975). *Power and the Corporate Mind*. Boston: Houghton-Mifflin.

Index

Printed and bound by CPI Group (UK) Ltd, Croydon, CR0 4YY